HINTS ON THE STUDY
OF
The Bhagavad-Gita

HINTS ON THE STUDY OF The Bhagavad-Gita.

BY

ANNIE BESANT.

GYAN

Published by

GYAN

Gyan Publishing House
5, Ansari Road
Daryaganj, New Delhi-110002
Phone: 011-47034999, 9811692060
E-mail: books@gyanbooks.com

Distribution Network
gyanbooks.com
India, USA, Canada, UK, Australia

ISBN: 978-93-6208-554-2 (HB)
First Published, 1906

2nd Impression 2024

Printed at: Gyan Press, Delhi.

HINTS ON THE STUDY OF THE BHAGAVAD-GITA
Author: ANNIE BESANT

HINTS ON THE STUDY

OF

The Bhagavad-Gita.

FOUR LECTURES DELIVERED AT THE THIRTIETH ANNIVERSARY MEETING OF THE THEOSOPHICAL SOCIETY AT ADYAR, MADRAS, DECEMBER, 1905.

BY

ANNIE BESANT.

Theosophical Publishing Society:

BENARES and LONDON.

Theosophist Office, Adyar.

1906.

CONTENTS.

—:o:—

THE BHAGAVAḌ-GÎṬÂ.

FIRST LECTURE.

THE GREAT UNVEILING.

BROTHERS:

IN trying to speak to you on four successive mornings on the matter of the *Bhagavaḍ-Gîṭâ*, I feel, more strongly than it is possible for any one of you to feel, my utter inadequacy for the task. To speak of the *Gîṭâ* is to speak of the history of the world, of its vast complexity, of that web of desires, thoughts, and actions which makes up the evolution of humanity; for the book is not simply the story of the teaching of Arjuna by Shrî Kṛiṣhṇa—it is far more than that. And all that one can pray in taking up a task so far beyond one's powers is that that flute, whose music compelled melody even from the very stones that heard it, may breathe the same all-compelling music in the heart of speaker and hearers alike; so that out of that music some note may echo in the hearts that are gathered here, to breathe over the lives that spring from those hearts something of the spirit embodied in the *Gîtâ* words. How great is the Song of the Lord, all nations with one voice acclaim. Not only in its own native land, but over all lands, that music has gone, and in every country has awakened some echo in receptive hearts. And yet, many a one who reads it, and would fain understand it, finds it—as indeed did the first hearer—difficult, complex and even confusing, flying apparently from one subject to another, speaking now of one method and then of a method apparently opposed, sometimes seeming to give counsel along one line and then counsel along another, speaking of the necessity of the life that is embodied in all beings, and yet with a continual refrain, "fight," by which the life was loosened from many a form. He who can understand the complexity of the *Gîtâ* can understand likewise the complexity of the world in which the author of the *Gîtâ* is the upholding and the sustaining life, and complex as the world is the *Gîtâ*, both worthy of the profoundest study.

But in these modern days the study is a difficult one, for the way of the Divine Teacher is not the way of the human pedagogue. God does not teach as man teaches, in text-books written for a boy to learn, exercising his memory rather than unfolding his life. Nature, which is the outer reflection of Deity, does not teach us by precept after precept, by spoken words easy to understand; and so, you notice that in the *Gîtâ*, where the method of teaching is that of the Divine Teacher and not that of the pedagogue, there is much confusion, much difficulty; and almost vexation shows itself, from time to time, in the heart and even on the lips of the learner. How often, during the earlier lessons, does the pupil bitterly complain to the Teacher that he cannot understand. How often comes out the bitter, reproachful, cry for teaching clear, definite and unmistakable. You must recall shloka after shloka in which the confusion of Arjuna shows itself, sometimes in pleading, sometimes in almost petulant, words: "I ask Thee which may be the better—that tell me decisively. I am thy disciple, suppliant to Thee; teach me" (ii. 7). And the answer? A long discourse, eloquent, beautiful, full of profoundest wisdom; but, after that discourse, what the result on the mind of the listener? "With these perplexing words Thou only confusest my understanding. Therefore tell me with certainty the one way by which I may reach bliss" (iii. 2). Again the Teacher speaks. Shloka after shloka, in musical beauty, flow from the Divine lips; and again, after two long discourses have been spoken, the same desperate cry: "Of the two which one is the better? That tell me conclusively" (v. i). How strange! Here is Shrî Kṛiṣhṇa teaching Arjuna, and yet He cannot make him understand. Here is the ideal pupil, the ideal disciple, crying aloud for light to his Master, and the light is not given. Ah no! It is not so. It is not the Master who refuses the light; it is the disciple who is not able to see by it, to understand. For the pupil is needed as well as the teacher, the receptive mind as well as the wisdom that flows from the divine lips. Of what avail the white splendour of the Sun, if it fall on eyes that are blind to its radiance? of what avail the melody of the most exquisite vînâ, if it fall on ears that are deaf, and cannot hear? The difficulty, my brothers, lies with us and not with Those who teach. They pour out floods of Divine Wisdom, but can the ocean empty itself into a tiny pail? What we see is the grudging, as it almost seems to us, on the part of the teacher; the pupil is eager for light, longing for knowledge, praying for Wisdom, and it does not come. Nay it comes, in floods overpowering—wave after wave sweeps over us, but we are dull and blind and senseless as the stones; nay, worse than stones, for they answer to the melody of the flute, and we answer not.

Now this is the first great lesson of the *Gîtâ*.

That the pupil must make himself. You can learn all the outer things that man can teach by outer teaching, though even there the power of the pupil must condition the illumination the mind receives, and the instruction to him consists only of that which he assimilates. But of the Divine Wisdom you cannot learn one syllable, nay, one letter, until you live it in life, and not only repeat it with the lips. To understand the *Gîṭâ* you must live it, and, as you learn to live it, slowly the great meaning will dawn upon your intelligence; only as, step by step, the living is accomplished is the profound unveiling of the mysteries possible for the individual heart. And so, some will take up the *Gîṭâ* and read it through, and say: "It is very beautiful, but after all there is nothing in it, which we did not know before." And others will read, and read, and read, and the reading bears but little fruit. Well, but you may say, it is taught in some of our Shâsṭras that if you read so much, a quarter of a shloka, half a shloka, a shloka, or a quarter of the whole book itself, such and such will be the fruits. Aye, but the reading that brings the fruit of knowledge is not the reading of the eye but the reading of the life; and the man who sees, the man who reads, a quarter of a shloka, and reads it in such a manner that it becomes part of his life, so that all around him may also read it in his life, and know that in that man so much of the *Gîtâ* has found embodiment, that man has truly read it, and he reaps the fruit. Each true reading marks a stage of human evolution, marks a point in human progress. It is not the mere repetition of the words; it is the mighty indwelling spirit, incarnate in our hearts, that manifests the fruit.

Now in this *Bhagavaḍ-Gîtâ* there are two quite obvious meanings, distinct and yet closely connected the one with the other, and the method of the connection it is well to understand. First the historical. Now, specially in modern days when western thought is so much swaying and colouring the eastern mind, Indians as well as Europeans are apt to shrink from the idea of historical truths being conveyed in much of the sacred literature; those enormous periods, those long reigns of Kings, those huge and bloody battles, surely they are all simple allegory, they are not history. But what is history, and what is allegory? History is the working out of the plan of the LOGOS, His plan, His scheme for evolving humanity; and history is also the story of the evolution of a World-Logos, who will rule over some world-system of the future. That is history, the life-story of an evolving Logos in the working out of the plan of the ruling LOGOS. And when we say allegory, we only mean a smaller history, a lesser history, the salient points of which, reflections of the larger history, are repeated in the life-story of each individual Jîvâṭmâ, each individual embodied Spirit. History, seen from the true standpoint, is the plan of the ruling LOGOS for the evolution of a future Logos, manifested in all planes and visible to us on the physical, and therefore full of profoundest interest and full of profoundest meaning. The inner meaning, as it is sometimes called, that which comes home to the hearts of you and me, that which is called the allegory, is the perennial meaning, repeated over and over again in each individual, and is really the same in miniature. In the one, Îshvara lives in His world, with the future Logos and the world for His body; in the other He lives in the individual man, with the Jîvâṭmâ and its vehicles for His body. But, in both, are the one Life and the one Lord, and he who understands either understands the twain. None, save the wise, can read the page of history with eyes that see; none, save the wise, can trace in their own unfolding the mighty unfolding of the system in which a future Logos Himself is the Jîvâṭmâ, and that ruling LOGOS is the Supreme Self; and inasmuch as the lesser is the reflection of the greater, inasmuch as the history of the evolving individual is but a poor faint copy of the evolving of the future Logos, therefore in the scriptures there is ever what we call a double meaning—

that history which shews a greater Self evolving, and the inner allegorical meaning that tells of the unfolding of the lesser Selves. We cannot afford to lose either meaning, for something of the richness of the treasure will thus escape us; and you must have steadily and clearly in mind that it is no superstition of the ancients, no dream of the fore-fathers, no fancy of the ignorant generations of far-off antiquity, that saw in the little lives of men reflections of the greater Life that has the Universe for its expression. Nor should you wonder, nor be perplexed, when you catch, now and again, in that unfolding picture, glimpses of things that on a smaller scale are familiar in your own evolving; and instead of thinking that a myth is a cloudy something which grows out of the history of a far-off individual, exaggerated and enlarged, as is the modern fancy, learn that what *you* call myth is the truth, the reality, the mighty unfolding of the Supreme Life which causes the shaping of a Universe, and that what *you* call history, the story of individuals, is only a poor faint copy of that unfolding. When you see the likeness, learn that it is not the great that is moulded by the small; it is the minute that is the reflection of the mighty. And so, in reading the *Bhagavaḍ-Gîtâ*, you can take it as history; and then it is the Great Unveiling, that makes you understand the meaning and the purpose of human history, and thus enables you to scan, with eyes that see, the panorama of the great unfolding of events in nation after nation, and in race after race. He who thus reads the *Gîtâ* in human history can stand unshaken amid the crash of breaking worlds. And you can also read it for your own individual helping and encouraging and enlightening, as an allegory, the story of the unfolding Spirit within yourselves. And I purpose, this morning, to take these two meanings as our special study, and to show how the *Gîtâ* as history is the Great Unveiling, the drawing away of the veil that covers the real scheme which history works out on the physical plane; for it was that which removed the delusion of Arjuna and made him able to do his duty at Kurukshetra. And then, turning from that vaster plane, to seek its meaning as it touches the individual unfolding of the Spirit, we shall see what that has of teaching for us, what that means for us of individual illumination, for just as history is true, so is allegory true. As the history, as we shall see, was the preparation for the India of the present, and the preparation for the India of the future, so also is that true which is elsewhere written in the *Mahâbhârata*: "I am the Teacher, and the mind is my pupil." From that standpoint we shall see Shrî Krishna as the Jagat Guru, the World Guru, and Arjuna as the mind,

Lower Manas, taught by the Teacher. And thus we may learn to understand its meaning for ourselves in our own little cycle of human growth.

Now, an Avaṭâra is the Îshvara, the LOGOS, of a world-system, appearing in some physical form at some great crisis of evolution. The Avaṭâra descends—unveils Himself would be a truer phrase; "descends" is when we think of the Supreme as though far-off, when truly He is the all-pervasive Life in which we live; to the outer eye only is it a coming down and descending—and such an Avaṭâra is Shrî Kṛishṇa. He comes as the LOGOS of the system, veiling Himself in human form, so that He may, as man, outwardly shape the course of history with mighty power, as no lesser force might avail to shape it. But the Avaṭâra is also the Îshvara of the human Spirit, the Logos of the Spirit, the Supreme Self, the Self of whom the individual Spirit is a portion—an amsha. Avaṭâra, then, as the Îshvara of our system; Avaṭâra, also, as the Îshvara of the human Spirit; and as we see Him in these two presentments, the light shines out and we begin to understand.

Let us take the historical drama, the setting of the great teaching. India had passed through a long cycle of greatness, of prosperity. Shrî Râma Chanḍra had ruled over the land as the model of the Divine Kingship that guides, shapes, and teaches an infant civilisation. That day had passed. Others had come, feebler to rule and guide, and many a conflict had taken place. The great Kṣhaṭṭriya caste had been cut down almost to the root by the Avaṭâra Parashurâma, Râma of the axe; it had again grown up, strong and vigorous. Into that India the new manifestation came. In that past of her story, this first offshoot of the great Âryan Race had settled in the northern parts of India. It had there served as the model, the world-model, for a nation. That was its function. A religion, embracing the heights and depths of human thought, able to teach the ryot in his field, able to teach the philosopher and the metaphysician in his secluded study, a world-embracing religion, had been proclaimed through the lips of the Ṛiṣhis of this first offshoot of the Race. Not only a religion, but also a polity, an economic and social order, planned by the wisdom of a Manu, ruled at first by that Manu Himself. Not only a religion and a polity, but also the shaping of the individual life on the wisest lines—the successive Varṇas, the successive Âshramas; the stages of life, in the long life of the individual, were marked in the castes, and each caste-life of the embodied Jîvâṭmâ reproduced in its main principles, in the individual life, the Âshramas through which a man passed between birth and death. Thus perfectly thought out, thus marvelously planned, this infant civilisation was given to the Race as a world-model, to show what might be done where Wisdom ruled and Love inspired.

The word spoken out by that ancient model was the word Dharma—Duty, Fitness, Right Order. Gradually, like all things human, it deteriorated, and grew weaker and weaker. It had done its work, in building up for the world a model, from which the younger nations of the world might take what parts they could, and build them into their own civilisations.

Another function, grander, diviner, more wonderful, was now to come to the sacred Eastern Land, and it was to prepare it for that function that Shrī Kṛiṣhṇa wrought out the change. India, that had been a world-model of ordered duty in her divinely-moulded peoples, was in the far off future—which to His divine eyes was not distant, for what is distance to the Deity to whom past and future are but one eternal present?—to serve not as world-model but as World-Saviour; that is the key to the later events. No nation may come to such high office save by treading the valley of the shadow of death, and by drinking to the very dregs the bitter cup of humiliation; for that Shrī Kṛiṣhṇa came—to make it possible, and to make it inevitable. No hands less wise and less loving than those of an Avaṭāra might start the Indian nation on the path, the bitter path of humiliation and of suffering. And this dominates—as you will see if you read His life-story carefully—this dominates His policy right through. He never swerves, He never changes. All His work, into which He throws His matchless power, is guided by this far-sighted, unswerving, changeless, will. The changeless will is there, in whatever veil of mâyâ He may, for the time, enwrap Himself. He wills to shape this land, this race, to be a World-Saviour. What does the shaping mean? It means first humiliation; and has not India passed through humiliation after humiliation? Who can look back to her as she existed in the splendour of her past, and see her empress of the worlds of spirit and of mind, with her triple crown of spiritual knowledge, of intellectual power, and of prosperity unbounded, and then, looking around to-day, see her discrowned, without tears, tears of the very heart, more like to drops of blood? And yet, the Lord of Love on Kurukşheţra made that very destiny possible which to-day we see; nay, made it inevitable. He broke into pieces the hard wall of steel, wrought of the swords of her Kşhaţţriya caste; He slew them by their own sharp swords, this, the mighty Lord of All, for He had come as time of doom:

Time am I, laying desolate the world,

Made manifest on earth to slay mankind;

Not one of all these warriors ranged for strife
Escapeth death. (xi. 32).

The hour had struck; the swords of the Kṣhaṭṭriyas shivered against each other in fratricidal strife. The bodies of the Kṣhaṭṭriyas were left corpses on the plain of Kurukṣheṭra. The struggle for a kingdom resulted in the dissolution of two kingdoms, and modern India was born. The forehead with the triple crown was cast down into the dust, so that the destroying waves of invasion might sweep over her time after time. Alexander came, and swept over the northern lands, and his armies rolled back again to Greece, enriched with eastern thought. Still bitterer the passion, still more cruel the humiliation, when wave after wave of the northern Asian nations, from Mongolia, from Turkestan, holding the fiercest form of the faith of Islâm, the Islâm of the sword not of the pen, rolled over her and strove to overwhelm the faith of the Hindu people, and the Moghal throne was set up on the very site where Yuḍhiṣthiṛa had reigned. Later still, one European nation after another played with the dice of war and commerce for the ruling of India. Her embankments were gone. No warriors or armaments, however heroic, were strong enough to stem the flood; the waves of the ocean of invasion swept from coast to coast and submerged the whole. It was the hour of her passion, of her crucifixion among the nations.

Lifted high upon her cross of pain, jeered at and mocked, derided and scorned, her robes of beauty the spoil of the contemptuous soldiery, she has hung there, dying, these many hundred years. But when you have told of the humiliation and the passion, of the crucifixion and the wounding, you have told only half the story of a World-Saviour; for after the passion comes the resurrection, as inevitably as day follows night. And if you look with clear-eyed vision, unblinded by the tears provoked by that story of the humiliation and the passion, you will see that as each wave of conquest swept over the land, it fertilised the land, it did not really destroy it. And each wave, on rolling back, carried back with it something wherewith to fertilise its own land, and left in India some new thought, some fresh idea, some treasure to enrich her ever-growing thought. A destructive flood it seemed, when you looked at it from the outer side of invasion. A fertilising flood it was known to be, looked at from the inner side, like the Nile that floods Egypt so that all the land seems drowned, but on that flood the crops of the coming season depend. For does not the Avaṭâra guide the world, and out of seeming evil, He brings unceasing good. And because He loves, and is wise as well as loving, with unswerving hands He guides His chosen through the valley of misery and the hell of humiliation, in order that, purified by suffering and enriched by the experience gathered from many nations who came to mingle with her own, the World-Saviour might arise glorious on the morning of resurrection, to shed new light over the whole world, instead of the light being shed on one nation only.

Such was the meaning of the coming of Shrî Kṛiṣhṇa, and such the work that the Avaṭâra saw before Him, and with unchanging will steadfastly carried out. But herein lies for us another lesson, for we observe that in carrying out the end, He never forgot or failed to use the means which Right Order demanded at the time. Do you remember how, before the battle-day dawned, Shrî Kṛiṣhṇa went to the court of the King Dhṛiṭaraṣhtra, and how with His matchless eloquence, His golden tongue, He pleaded there for peace? You remember how He called Duryoḍhana, how against his obstinacy He matched His patience, and against his mad folly His own sweet wisdom; how mild His words, how tactful His suggestions; nay, when all else had failed, even a partial unveiling of His form as Îshvara, in order that He might strive to the uttermost to carry conviction to the hearts opposed to Him and bent on fatal war. So many efforts for peace, and yet He knew that war was inevitable. Such striving after the unattainable, such endeavourings to bring about things which would have frustrated His own mission. How strange that seems to our purblind eyes. But how necessary, and how wise when we begin to see. For although He knew that those efforts would fail in the purpose of the moment, though He knew that war was inevitable and Himself willed that war, and was resolute to bring it about, none the less He knew that duty must be performed, and it was His duty as patriot and as statesman to strive for peace with every effort and with every human power He possessed. He knew in His divine wisdom that the value of effort does not lie in the immediate success, as success may be counted by you and me; that efforts, directed to noble ends, are never lost, but are an ever-accumulating force, and that the future success could not work itself out correctly and perfectly, if one of those efforts were lacking, if one of those struggles were not made. He knew the secret of all action. He knew that right action is not wrought by the wise for the immediate and apparent fruit of action; that right action ought always to be performed, even though inevitable failure waits to meet it, and He well knew that all those efforts of His were forces, energies, necessary to bring about the ultimate result in what is still to us the far-off future. Those efforts for peace made by Shrī Kṛiṣhṇa, frustrated as they seemed to be at the time by the wilfulness of Ḍuryoḍhana, those efforts are part of the energies that are making for peace universal in the future, when the need for the lessons of war will be over, and the white wings of peace will brood over a world at rest. And so He worked, and so He strove.

Now to the story, the bird's-eye-view having been taken. Arjuna, when the day of battle dawned, seated in the white-horsed chariot, with the Charioteer divine beside him, felt his heart fail him, as well it might. Friends on either side; relatives arrayed under hostile banners; nay, his old teachers, Bhīṣhma, Ḍroṇa, and the rest, ranged against him and guiding the enemy's arms; what heart would not fail in such a conflict of duty? There must be a battle within the heart to be fought out before the battle of Kurukṣheṭra, and, as this battle raged, he was ill at ease, despondent, confused as to ḍharma. What ought he to do? Was Kingship sufficient reward for the slaying of the loved ones? Would the crown sit soft upon the brow when the heart was broken? Nay, with true prevision, he saw the heavy burden of misery awaiting conqueror as well as conquered, the shadow of the coming day, when in the empty court, he would seek in vain for the faces of his beloved kinsmen, the playfellows of the dear childish days; that shadow descended in its obscurity and darkened his loving heart. "How shall I kill these?" he cried, "my Gurus how shall I slay? better to eat the beggar's crust as exile, than to slay these Gurus high-minded, these relatives beloved. My very food would taste of blood" (ii. 46). And his whole argument was a reasonable argument; his ideas of caste-confusion, his ideas of the gradual decay of ḍharma, which would inevitably follow the slaughter on Kurukṣheṭra, were all correct. History has justified them; his forebodings have proved true; ḍharma *has* decayed; caste-confusion *is* here. His vision was not, then, a blinded vision, only it did not see far enough. He saw the immediate future clearly, distinctly, rightly. Is it not true that ḍharma has decayed? Is it not true that we have now complete caste-confusion? What has become of the ḍharma of caste? It has vanished, as Arjuna feared it would. His words from the standpoint of a limited vision were truly "words of wisdom" (ii. 11), of worldly wisdom, the wisdom of the unilluminated mind. He saw with true prevision that which was coming on the land. He understood that he was engaged in a work which meant ruin for India; that he knew, though he could not see beyond the India of the moment; the mightier India which was to be born of the birth-throes of the ruin was beyond his ken. What wonder that it should be so, what marvel? How could we expect Arjuna, wise in much as he was, to pierce through the dim mists of the future, and to see what was to be born out of this temporary misery? How could we expect him to see the result—the true result of all the struggle? Why then was he so sharply rebuked? If his prophecy were true, if his prevision were correct, if ḍharma was going to fade away, and castes would become confused, why did these words of rebuke fall from the divine lips? "Whence hath this dejection befallen thee in this perilous strait, ignoble, heaven-closing, infamous, O Arjuna? Yield not to impotence, O Pârṭha! It doth not befit thee. Shake off this paltry faint-heartedness. Stand up, Paranṭapa" (ii. 2, 3). Why that strong rebuke? Because the plan, the scheme, of Îshvara must be carried out, at whatever cost for the moment, by those who are His agents in the work. Arjuna had been living with Shrî Kṛiṣhna since he was a youth, and was His dearest friend. As youth, you remember, how they met after that great tournament where Arjuna won Ḍraupaḍi, stood as conqueror on the field. You remember how they grew up side by side, how the influence, the marvellous influence, of Shrî Kṛiṣhṇa had, for all these years, been round His chosen friend, preparing him for the great part that in the struggle he was to play. There was a plan to be worked out, in which Arjuna was an actor, to which his eyes were blind. He was under a delusion; confused, perplexed, he could not see; and that great plan that had to be worked out was changeless; nothing that Arjuna could do would alter it, no resistance of his might avail to make it different from what it was. He was to understand that forms lose life, but that the Spirit dieth never, and that when the work of the form is over, it is well that it should be shattered into pieces; that only when the Spirit shapes for itself new forms can the larger unfolding take place. He who hesitates to destroy the form when its work is done knows not the power of the life that is the builder, and shall continue to build in days to come.

None the less is it true that in the crash of systems whose work is over, it is those who perform the Sahajan Ḍharma—the inborn duty—who serve as the bridge from the old order to the new. Those who understand the necessary progression of events, those who know that forms must break when the new forms are ready for birth, those who steadfastly perform the ḍharma of the older forms into which they were born, although they know them to be dying, until the new are ready, form the bridge over which the ignorant may walk in safety amid the crash of a falling system into a new system prepared by the Spirit that ever renews the life and builds new forms. So that Arjuna had to do his duty, no matter what the outcome might be, no matter what the result; and, strangely enough, the man who was chosen for this great duty—to be the bridge to the new order—was one in whose own family this very same fact of caste-confusion was very definitely manifested. For you will remember, if you think back over the story of Arjuna, that his great-grand-mother was a fisher-maiden married to a King; that that King's sons died childless, and that Vyâsa was called in, in order to raise up children to be the heirs of the monarch who was dead. And of these children, thus born, Pâṇdu had so acted that he too was not the father of his so-called sons, who were born of Kunṭi and Maḍri by the touch of Ḍevas. Thus alike from the great-grand-mother, the fisherman's daughter, and from the grand-mother, who bore not child to her own lord but to Vyâsa, and from the mother, who was overshadowed by Ḍevas, there were the mingling of strange and diverse currents in the veins of this Arjuna, chosen friend of Shrî Kṛishṇa, chosen tool for the work of transition. On which facts the thoughtful may fitly ponder.

But I said that it was necessary that the divine plan of evolution should be carried out, whether Arjuna willed it, or whether he willed it not; and so it is declared as to the great scheme: "The

Lord dwelleth in the hearts of all beings, O Arjuna, by His illusive power causing all things to revolve as though mounted on a potter's wheel" (xviii. 61). The scheme is there; there is no choice, no power of change; wisdom is not to be corrected by ignorance, nor the vision that pierces the future to be taught to see aright by blinded eyes. The scheme could not be changed for Arjuna's feelings; the scheme was not to be altered because Arjuna's heart might be broken in the carrying of it out. The time was ripe; the hour had struck. "Time am I" (xi.32), now and here present, and it was too late to hesitate; the time for thought was past; the time for action had arrived. Nay, with his past dharma behind him forcing him on, with a duty upon him which he was bound to discharge by virtue of the causes he had set going in the past, he had not even the power to refuse to play his part, chosen by him in his past; and this Shrî Kṛiṣhṇa tells him in clear, plain words: "Entrenched in egoism, thou thinkest, 'I will not fight'; to no purpose thy determination; nature will constrain thee. O son of Kuntî, bound by thine own duty, born of thine own nature, that which from delusion thou desirest not to do, even that helplessly thou shalt perform" (xviii. 59, 60). What does that mean? It means that in the great crisis of a nation's fate when the Lord, mounted on the potter's wheel, is turning the wheel of history; no hand may then avail to stay it; that those who have chosen the leading parts by countless choices in their past, have generated a force of karma behind them which they, in their present bodies, are unable to resist, and that the Kṣhaṭṭriya blood which ran in the veins of Arjuna, the power also of physical heredity from generations behind him who had done Kṣhaṭṭriya duty face to face with the foe, would carry him away even against his present wish, against his present heart, against his present will; the mighty power of the inborn nature created by his past would carry him, despite his present self, into the midst of an opposing army, and helplessly he would fight, constrained by his own past. But if he fought in that way, evil was it for him. The plan of Îshvara indeed would be carried out; the potter's wheel revolving would not stop; the Lord mounted there could not be checked by the minute power of Arjuna on Kurukṣheṭra. But for Arjuna, forced helplessly into the struggle, ill indeed would it be if, entrenched in that egoism of the moment's feeling, he still persisted, "I will not fight." "If from egoism thou wilt not listen, thou shalt be destroyed utterly" (xviii. 58). There is God's purpose and man's co-operation, told you in a few sentences. The great plan you cannot change; the opportunity is given you to co-operate; but, if driven by your past to co-operation and resisting in the present by egoism, by thinking yourself the actor instead of yielding yourself as a tool in the great Dramatist's hand, you say: "I will not fight; I will not do my duty; I will not perform my task;" then, in spite of the unwilling performance, you shall be utterly destroyed; for your present choice is then to fail in your duty, and the inner choice determines the future as the past choice the present. The plan shall be triumphant, but the egoism in which you took refuge shall destroy you, even while you are forced into outer obedience to the plan.

Thus to Arjuna was made the great unveiling, and his attitude to the outer world is changed. He understands now what history means. He realises the unchanging plan, and the part in it of the individual selves, who have made themselves worthy to co-operate with the mighty Lord. He knows now that Shrî Krishna is Time—Time made manifest to destroy these peoples. "Therefore fight." Just because the time has come when, for the good of all humanity, these obstructive objects must be swept away, "therefore fight." "Be thou the outward cause" (xi. 33), the sword, the tool. It is as though He said: "I have in reality slain them, and slaying only means their liberation. They now form obstacles, hindrances. Death is their friend, their liberator, and is not their foe. Dying, they come to Me, their living Lord. They fling themselves into My mouth (xi. 26—29), and their bodies perish that their true life may grow. Contribute then to the great task, and liberate these who are living Spirits, while the obstructing bodies fall. Because I am Time, because the scheme is sure, because the end is certain, therefore fight." Arjuna understood. Listen to his last words: " Destroyed is my delusion. I have gained knowledge through Thy grace, O immutable one. I am firm, my doubts have fled away. I will do according to Thy word" (xviii. 73). He had learnt what history means. He had learnt the place of the plan and the place of the actor. He realised that it was not he at all who wrought, save as the tool of the all-wise, of the all-loving; no longer he thought of friends or enemies, no longer thought of personal ties, of personal attachments. In the wonder of that world-unveiling teaching he realises the one Lord who moves all, who works ever for the best, by the shortest possible road; and, seeing that, he throws himself joyfully at His feet to do according to His word. "Destroyed is my delusion." "I will fight." And so in all history, if only we can see aright, in the history around us as in the history of Arjuna on Kurukṣhetra; if we can learn the spirit of the great unveiling, the meaning of the life behind the veil and of the little lives on this side, their co-operation, their relations the one to the other, then in every struggle we can throw ourselves on the right side, and fight without doubt, without illusion, without fear, for the Warrior who really fights is doing all, and we are but the cells in His body, with our wills harmonised into unity with His. The clearing away of illusion is necessary, in order that activity may not be paralysed by doubt, doubt, the most fatal enemy of action. Doubt saps virility, vampirises the mind. Necessary, absolutely necessary, as a stage to knowledge, it breaks the healthy link between thought and action when it is unduly prolonged, and becomes a habitual atmosphere. "The ....doubting self goeth to destruction; nor this world, nor that beyond, nor happiness, is there for the doubting self" (iv. 40). "Therefore fight" is the constant refrain. Understand in order that you may act.

That is the unveiling of history. I have no time to work it out more fully, but you see the principle underlying the whole; apply it to the struggles of the nations that go on round you at the present moment. Look through the veil to the reality behind it, and you will see everywhere the great Avaṭâra guiding, and all things are very well planned, and are working towards a foreseen end.

That is the historical lesson; and what is the

other lesson, the lesson of the allegory? Conflict, evidently, between the Lower Manas, the mind unfolding, symbolised by Arjuna, and Kâma, the passional nature, symbolised by the relatives, headed by Ḍuryoḍhana, embodying all the ties of the past. Arjuna stands there as the Lower Manas, unilluminated, doubtful, wavering, questioning, first moving this way then the other, unsure of itself, always asking questions, and when answered, not understanding the answer, always puzzled as to what was really the best. So much this way, but just as much on the other side; this argument is very good, but this argument also is admirable; between the two always swaying backwards and forwards, first to one side then to the other. We have here a type of Manas unilluminated, and to that mind the Teacher spoke the words of wisdom just quoted: "Nor this world, nor that beyond, nor happiness, is there for the doubting self." A self that is ever doubting and cannot make up his mind; who, the moment a question is decided, sees all the arguments on the other side and wants to begin over again to go through the whole, makes no progress. It is the exaggeration of the virtues of caution and prudence, the exaggeration of a virtue which becomes a vice. Better act and make a blunder, and thus learn how to do better action in the future, than ever hesitate to act at all. For the paralysing doubt prevents you from gaining the lessons which experience alone can teach you. The hesitation comes out strongly in all the arguments of Arjuna. The urging to decisiveness comes out strongly in the words of the Teacher. The stages through which Arjuna has to go we can recognise in our own experience. First, in his youth, Arjuna, a lad of the court, is subject to the elders of the household in all earlier stages of his growth; wisely and necessarily subject, for by such subjection alone can mind be induced to overcome its inertia and exert itself, and by that exertion unfold its powers. And in the early days of evolution thus it is with humanity. Under the tutelage of the elders, and following without hesitation the impulses born of natural appetite and pleasures, the mind pursues its course without much thought and without hesitation or doubt; there is no struggle. Then comes the time of struggle belonging to the intermediate stages, when it is seen that the gratification of natural impulses, of Kâma, is unsatisfying; that the gratification of Kâma brings misery as well as happiness; when it is seen that disappointments and frustrations tread on the heel of gratified desires, and a longing arises to understand. Then comes the time of struggle, the time of warfare, of misery, of doubt; the mind is confused as to ḍharma, confused as to which path is the better. The mind cries to the teacher for help, and the answer only bewilders, because Manas is not yet ready to see the truth, but is confused with all the attractions around, to which the heart is drawn; the truth seems dry, hard, repellent; to follow it seems to slay all the joys of life, nay, life itself. Then comes the vision of the Supreme, that which alone takes away the taste for the pleasures yielded by the objects around us; only when the Supreme is seen, when the fuller life suffuses the lesser, does the attractiveness of the life of the senses depart (ii. 59). Then Manas arises triumphant, illuminated with the light of the Self, clear, radiant, decided; the delusion is destroyed, the warrior is the conqueror over his foes, Parantapa.

This is, in truth, the path of the warrior soul; this is, in truth, the way along which the warrior soul must go. Friends on both sides; for when on the Kurukshetra of the soul begins the battle which is to bring final victory, illumination, union with the Supreme, never are all the friends that grow out of the ties of the past, found on one side; friends are on both sides, warring the one against the other. There press in conflicting claims, conflicting duties, conflicting obligations of every sort; it is not enough to wish to do the right; it is easy to act when you know: the difficulty is to see the road amid the din and dust of the battle, and to have the sight keen enough to pierce the clouds and to see where the path of duty lies. Friends on both sides—how shall they be renounced? Nay, more then friends must the warrior soul find among his opponents. Teachers, Gurus, those to whom in the past the warrior had looked for help, for guidance—Bhîshma and Droṇa, types of those who help and guide and teach. The elders are against him; the friends and relations, they also are against him; and those that are lesser also, the younger, criticising, ignorantly blaming and despising; the warrior soul has to stand alone, as Arjuna stood in the empty space between the armies. Alone, and yet not alone, for the Teacher was beside him, the divine Charioteer was there; the Self, awaiting recognition. Into the battle he must plunge alone; by his strong right arm, by his own unflinching will, by his own unwavering courage, that battle must be fought to the bitter end. He feels himself isolated to the very uttermost power of isolation. And in that isolation, that loneliness, it is that he must find the Self. There, in the midst of the struggle, when he is alone, when all are against him, the glory of the Self shines forth upon him, and he knows verily that he is not alone; in spite of the wounds, the blood from which was blinding him, in spite of the dinted armour, the soiled garments, and the broken weapons, the warrior soul has stood undaunted to the end, knowing not that the shield of his Teacher had been over him in the moment of the worst peril, knowing not that when there came against him the one missile that no human strength could meet, his Teacher had turned it against his own bosom, and it had changed into a garland on the neck of the Charioteer. He knew not of the invisible buckler that had turned aside the stream of fire, which the Lord alone could face; he knew not, thought not, dreamed not, that the Royal Warrior, veiled in the Charioteer, was shielding him; for had he felt that in the struggle, how should he have learned to trust the Self within? The Self without must vanish before the Self within is realised. That is the experience of every warrior soul; that is the experience that every one must pass through as he treads the path that leads to the Supreme; only in that uttermost loneliness of desolation can Arjuna, or any other, find the Self. Fear you not, then, who would be warriors, when friends blame and turn aside; fear you not even when elders condemn, when youngers despise, when equals scorn; go on undaunted, unflinching, for the Self is within you. You may make many blunders, for the Self is embodied—mistakes belong to the body; and remember that they are of the body, not of the Spirit within, and, by the suffering which follows those very mistakes, the grosser matter is burned up, and the Self becomes more manifest. Go on fighting, struggling, full of courage, with brave and undaunted heart, and, at the end of your battle on Kurukṣheṭra, for you too shall dawn the Self in His Majesty, destroyed shall be your delusion also, and you shall see your Lord as He is.

———:o:———

THE BHAGAVAḌ-GÎṬÂ.

SECOND LECTURE.

AS YOGA SHÂSṬRA.

BROTHERS :—

IN dealing with a book so complicated as the *Gîṭâ*, in so brief a space of time as we have at our disposal, it is necessary to carefully select the points which shall be dealt with to bring out of the book its central thoughts, its main instructions, and so give a synthetic whole, which may remain in the mind, and into which, by your own study, the various details may be fitted in orderly fashion. To-day the part of the subject that I propose to lay before you is the nature of the *Gîṭâ* in its essence, as a Yoga Shâsṭra, a Scripture of Yoga. Under this will come the question of activity, the nature of activity, its binding force, the method of escape from its bonds by Yoga; that will lead us to a consideration of what is meant by Yoga, what is mean by the Yogî; and, later on, we shall have to ask what means are there within our reach by which Yoga may be attained? But that latter part I shall leave for to-morrow and the next day, and to-day we shall deal only with the points I have just mentioned: the *Gîṭâ* as Yoga Shâsṭra, activity, its binding nature, the method of liberation by Yoga, the nature of Yoga, and, therefore, the character of the Yogî.

First of all let us realise very definitely that the *Bhagavaḍ-Gîṭâ*, in its very essence, is that which it is called at the end of each of the Aḍhyâyas, a Yoga Shâsṭra. Unless we can learn yoga from this volume, it will, for us, have failed in its purpose.

Now, this Scripture of Yoga is given by the Lord of Yoga Himself. The speaker is the Yogeshvara, the Lord of Yoga, and we read, towards the close, when all has been told, how he who listened to the whole dialogue says: "By the favour of Vyâsa I listened to this secret and supreme yoga, from the Lord of Yoga, Kṛiṣhṇa Himself, speaking before mine eyes" (xviii. 75). So that we have here the teaching of Yoga by Him who is Yogeshvara. "How may I know Thee, O Yogî?" (x.17) is the cry of Arjuna. As Yogî he is thinking of Him, and it is in answer to the question: "How may I know thee, O Yogî?" that the Divine Form is revealed—

a most significant fact as to the true meaning of Yoga, as we shall see a little later on. And we find also that Arjuna puts forward the prayer in detail: "Tell me again of thy yoga" (x. 18). That is the thing he is seeking in order that hesitation and illusion may be cleared away. "He who knows in essence that sovereignty and yoga of mine, he is harmonised by unfaltering yoga" (x. 7); and thus the prayer of the disciple to the Lord of Yoga is that he may realise the inner meaning of *yoga*; that is the very essence of the *Gîtâ*. It is that which in the *Gîtâ* we should learn.

But how does this yoga, or the teaching of yoga, consort with what is the object of the *Gîtâ* on the very face of it? For you remember that the speaker and the pupil are standing in the midst, between two armies which are just going to engage in battle. It is just as "the flight of missiles is about to begin" (i. 20), that despondency seizes on the heart of the heroic Arjuna. The whole object of everything said and done, as recounted within the covers of the *Gîtâ*, has but one motive: to give Arjuna heart and courage, to drive him into action, to force him, if need be, into battling; and the argument is continually interspersed with the constant refrain: "Therefore, fight." It matters not what the line of argument may have been. It may have been an argument exposing the nature of the Jîvâtmâ, the unborn, the undying, the perpetual, and the constant; after that exposition: "Therefore, fight" (ii. 18). It may have been a long philosophical argument, expounding the nature of the One and the Manifold, explaining the constitution of the worlds, explaining the One Life that pervades everything; at the end of the philosophy, again sounds out the refrain: "Therefore at all times think upon Me only, and fight" (vi. 7). Or it may be the teaching of devotion, the bidding of the disciple to surrender all actions to his Lord, and "with thy thoughts resting on the supreme Self......engage in battle" (iii. 30). When the vision of the divine Form is given: "Destroy then fearlessly. Fight!" (xi. 34.) And at the very end, when He bids Arjuna: "Merge thy mind in Me, be my devotee, sacrifice to Me," still the recurring idea sounds out in the question: "Has thy delusion, caused by unwisdom, been destroyed?" (xviii. 65, 72.) And the result of the whole is Arjuna's resolution to fight: "I will do according to thy word" (xviii. 73), and he plunges into the fray.

Now that is very curious at first sight, and very unexpected. Yoga is going to be taught, the perfect Yogî is to be trained, and, at every break of the argument and change of the subject, the refrain: "Therefore, fight," rings out on the astonished ear. "Gird thee for the battle" (ii. 38) is the command of the Lord of Yoga. Everywhere in this Scripture of Yoga, there is the urging to action of the most violent kind, as though in fighting were embodied, as we may say, the very quintessence of activity, the rush of it, the whirl of it, the turmoil of it, the din of it. How could you have activity more active than the activity in the battle-field of heroes? Yet it is there that yoga is to be mastered; it is there that Yogeshvara appears in all the plenitude of His power and His magnificence. Now, this naturally seems strange, and most strange of all, perchance, to the modern mind, and to the modern mind in India. For, in modern India, great activity and the practice of yoga by no means go hand in hand, as a rule. Nay, I have here seen men who claim to speak for Hindu orthodoxy, who claim to defend it against the teaching of the Theosophist, I have here seen it put forward that no man can be a yogî, unless he live far apart from men in cave or jungle or desert, unless he live in some recess of the mighty Himâlayas, or other mountain range, under the sacred sky of India. I have heard it said that no man can be a yogî who is in the midst of activity, working, labouring, endeavouring to help all good things that are in the world, and therefore worldly; that yoga means seclusion, silence, inaction. Such apparently is the idea of many a modern Indian, and it is a fact—the reason for which we shall see later—that in the course of evolution between and activity born of desire for objects of the world and that noble and ceaseless activity which arises only out of the longing to co-operate with Îshvara, the Supreme, there is an intermediate stage where action has become distasteful, as belonging to the world, and the higher lesson of "action in inaction" (iv. 18) has not yet been learned by the pupil. But the Lord of Yoga Himself sees yoga in a very different light from that which I have just described: "He that performeth such action as is duty, independently of the fruit of action, he is an ascetic, he is a yogî" (vi. 1). He goes even further than that, and He declares: "Yoga is skill in action" (ii.50). So that in the mind of the Lord of Yoga, yoga seems to have connoted something very very different from the modern idea of secluding yourself from men, from sitting in the cave or jungle isolated from men. That has its place, that has its part, in human evolution. It is a stage in human progress. But yoga, as taught by the Lord of Yoga, the supreme yoga, is something different from that. Man is here in the world for activity; the Creator of the world is the embodiment of Kriyâ, activity. Brahmâ represents Kriyâ, and there is no object in being in the physical universe at all except for the development of right activity, directed by right thought and right desire; all else leads up to that. The world is full of desirable objects, filled by Îshvara Himself with objects that awaken desire; Îshvara Himself is hidden within every object, giving to each object its attractive charm, its alluring power. We shall see presently that there is nothing in the whole world in which the Lord of the world is not embodied. And this vast array of desirable things is placed in the world by Îshvara Himself. He veils Himself in these objects by Mâyâ, and by this He awakens desire in these portions of Himself that He has placed here to grow from the divine seed into the divine Lord. Desire is awakened, aroused, strengthened, by the presence of all these objects of desire. And if desire had not a part to play in human evolution, then should we have been born into a world which was a desert, where there was no object to attract, where there was nothing to allure. But the presence of these pleasure-giving objects, and the presence of these pain-giving objects also, not only arouses attraction and repulsion in us, but also they arouse thought in us; for difficulties are placed between us and the objects of our desire, and thought is awakened within the Jîvâtmâ, in order that these difficulties may be either over-climbed or evaded. And as we trace the course of human evolution, we find that thought is stimulated by desire and that all the vigourous thought-activities, that we see in the men of the world around us, are thought-activities motived by desire, stimulated, urged, impelled by desire. Unless Îshvara has planned His universe very much amiss—and we often imagine in our wisdom that we could have planned it better, had it been left to us to arrange—there must be some meaning in the presence of these objects which arouse desire, some meaning in these difficulties in appropriating them that make the exertion of thought inevitable. Desire and thought make the motive and the guiding powers of action, and action comes after desire and after thought, and is their natural, inevitable result. That is a point on which, for a moment, we pause that we may realise it. But in order to understand the full scope of it, the tremendous force of the argument that lies therein, you must think over it step by step, detail after detail, until you learn the world as Yogeshvaṛa has planned it, and not as man fancies or imagines it ought to be. And thus thinking, you will come to realise that the whole thing is arranged in order that activity may be aroused, because as He tells us: "Action is superior to inaction" (iii. 8). Hence man is coaxed and allured, stimulated and goaded into action, and we must keep that thought firmly in mind, else the meaning of the *Gîtâ* will inevitably escape us.

Why is it that so much stress is laid by Shrî Kṛiṣhṇa upon action? The reason comes out very strongly when we turn to the third Aḍhyâya, where He speaks so much of action, the Aḍhyâya called "The Yoga of Action." All depends upon action: "From food creatures become; from rain is the production of food; rain proceedeth from sacrifice, sacrifice ariseth out of action; know thou that from Brahma action groweth" (iii. 14, 15). There is the chain of life. Creatures from food, food from rain, rain from sacrifice, sacrifice from action, action from Îshvara—the whole life of the world, the whole reproduction of beings, everything that makes a world, a manvantara in contradistinction to a pralaya, all that depends upon activity, is born of action. So that action cannot be quite so despicable a thing as the modern Indian is sometimes inclined to think. And it may be that we should rightly date the beginning of the decadence of India from the time when people lost sight of the right proportion between action and inaction, and when they began to look on action as a hindrance to spiritual life, instead of as its means, instead of as being the way thereto. For is it not written that: "For a Sage, who is seeking yoga, action is called the means" (vi. 3). But you say: "Finish the shloka." Certainly. "For the same Sage, when he is enthroned in yoga, serenity is called the means." But does serenity mean inaction? On the contrary, we read a little further and we find it said of the serene Sage: "Acting in harmony with Me, let him render all action attractive" (iii. 26); so that this teaching of the value of action goes on from step to step, action, serenity, serene action. The reason why activity is necessary is given us very fully in this same Chapter. For it is declared: "As the ignorant act from attachment to action, O Bharaṭa, so should the wise act without attachment, desiring the welfare of the world. Let no wise man unsettle the mind of ignorant people attached to action; but" as I just quoted, "acting in harmony with Me, let him render all action attractive"(iii. 25, 26).

The action of Îshvara Himself, on what does it rest? "There is nothing," He says as Shrî Kṛiṣhṇa, "in the three worlds, O Pârṭha, that should be done by Me, nor anything unattained that might be attained; yet I mingle in action. For if I mingled not ever in action, unwearied, men all around would follow my path, O son of Pṛiṭhâ. These worlds would fall into ruin, if I did not perform action; I should be the author of confusion of castes, and should destroy these creatures" (iii. 22-24). There, in truth, is the root of all right activity. Right activity is co-operation with Îshvara, with the LOGOS of the universe; that is the highest path, and to that all training, all effort, inevitably must tend—co-operation with the divine Will, acting in harmony with the Will that works most wisely for the supremest good. Whatever may happen to be the duty of the moment, that is to be done; fighting, if fighting happens to be the business of the time, passivity, if passivity be needful. If the time has come, in the course of the world's history, when large numbers of men, going along the path that is leading them downwards, have to be rescued from the downward path by striking away the body, hopelessly distorted, in order that the living Spirit may shape for itself a better body ready for higher ends, then to strike away the bodies may be the co-operation demanded. You look on death as something sad and terrible. You think of death, influenced by western thinking, it may be, as a foe, as an enemy of man; but death has other aspects than that of man's foe, my brothers. Nay, death is the friend and not the foe of man; it is he who opens the door of the prison-house, where the Spirit within is chafing at the barriers imposed by a past not well lived, not well thought out. And often death, which looked at from one side is terrible, is seen as the very gateway of birth into life, when looked at from the other. And when a man like Duryodhana, noble in many of his impulses, splendid in his courage, loving his people and intent on their welfare, when a man like that is going what we call hopelessly wrong, and opposing the divine Will, what more gracious messenger can love itself send him than death, that strikes away the blundering body and unveils the eyes of the Spirit? And when you realise that, you begin to understand that even war, with all its horrors, is a message of mercy, of rescue, of liberation, for many a one who may fall on the field of battle. And if the heart of God can bear to see the suffering, we, who are so much more selfish, may be able also to bear to see it, and be willing to co-operate with Him. And, therefore, if wisdom and love declare that fighting is necessary for progress at the moment, then fighting is co-operation with Ishvara, and the word of command comes: "Therefore fight, O Arjuna."

Right activity, then, is the lesson of the *Gita*, and right activity is acting in harmony with the divine Will. That is the only true definition of right activity; not for fruit, not for desire for movement, not from attachment to any object, or to any results of activity, but, wholly in harmony with the Will that works for universal good. "Without attachment, constantly perform action which is duty" (iii.19). That, and that only, is right activity.

Now comes a great difficulty in the midst of all this teaching. It may be true, and it is true, that the Jñânî, the man who is perfectly wise, the Bhakta, the man who is perfectly devoted, the Kartâ, the man who is acting in the right way, that all these men are working along real mârgas, real paths, towards the Supreme, and they all lead up to, and blend in, this right activity. For right activity perfect wisdom is needed, and perfect devotion, and perfect unattachment to the fruits of action, and only those who are wise, devoted and active can carry on right activity. What then is the difficulty? Because man is bound by action. This thought seems to have surged up in Arjuna's mind when he was listening to this glorification of activity. Man is bound by action, and seeing this difficulty the Teacher declares: "The world is bound by action" (iii. 9). Action forges bonds between us and the things to which the action is directed.] We tie ourselves up, whatever our deeds may be, good, bad or indifferent. It is not only evil action that binds; good action binds quite as much. True, the fruit is different. The fruit of evil action is sorrow, and the fruit of good action is happiness; but good and evil actions equally bind the man. "The world is bound by action." Then, in what kind of place are we? How is this problem to be solved? We are to be active, to work, to be busy, we are to throw ourselves into the life of the world, to make action attractive to others, and to work for the welfare of mankind; and all the time we are winding round our limbs chains that fetter, binding the wings of the Spirit, that fain would soar, by these continual bonds of activity which tie him down. Can that be the outcome of the teaching of the Lord of Yoga? No. It is quite true that man is bound by action. Nay, the Lord goes very much further than merely to say that man is bound by action. He seems to make things a little hopeless for us, as He goes on from one step to another in His argument; for not content with telling us that man is bound by action, He tells us also that: "Man winneth not freedom from action by abstaining from activity" (iii. 4). Here we have the first door of escape shut against us. We do not get rid of action by remaining inactive: "Nor by mere renunciation doth he rise to perfection" (iii. 4). The problem becomes more and more tangled as we go on. No wonder that Arjuna was confused. The Teacher presses it still further and further. That is not the whole. By inaction you cannot attain freedom, but you cannot really even be inactive. Even that is shut out: "Nor can any one, even for an instant, remain actionless; for helplessly is every one driven to action by the qualities born of nature" (iii. 5). As He says again in another passage: "Nor indeed can embodied beings completely relinquish action" (xviii. 11). What then is an unfortunate man to do? He is told he is not to be inactive. When he acts, he is told that action bind him. When he wishes to be free he is told he cannot abstain from action. Nay, he is told even something more. "By performing action without attachment, man verily reacheth the Supreme" (iii. 19). What a tangle of contradictions we seem to have got ourselves into. Are we always to remain bound to this wheel of births and deaths? Are we always to be slaves, bound by bonds that we have forged by our own activity? Is there no freedom for man? Is there no liberation for him? Is he always to be a hopelessly bound being, enslaved by the bonds that are born of action? Nay, the lesson goes further, and I stopped in the middle of the shloka when I read that: "The world is bound by action." "The world is bound by action, unless performed for the sake of sacrifice" (iii. 9). A gleam of light comes through the darkness. If action is performed as sacrifice, यज्ञार्थात् "for the sake of sacrifice," if it is offered as sacrifice, then it loses its binding power. Shrî Kṛiṣhṇa says still something more than that. "He who is free from the egoistic notion, whose reason is not affected, though he slay these peoples, he slayeth not, nor is bound" (xviii. 17). And again even something more: "Janaka and others," He says, "attained to perfection by action" (iii. 20). Then there is some kind of action which not only does not bind, but is, in itself, a means of liberation—again a thought which is not in harmony, as we well know, with some of the modern teachings, nor, indeed, with some which are regarded as authoritative. And yet it is put very emphatically, very strongly, with re-iteration: "Having thus known, our forefathers, ever seeking liberation, performed action; therefore do thou also perform action, as did our forefathers in the olden time......He who seeth inaction in action, and action in inaction, he is wise among men, he is harmonious, even while performing all action. Whose works are all free from the moulding of desire, whose actions are burned up by the fire of wisdom, him the wise have called a Sage. Having abandoned attachment to the fruit of action, always content, nowhere seeking refuge, he , doing anything, although doing actions. Hoping for naught, his mind and self controlled, having abandoned all greed, performing action by the body alone, he doth not commit sin. Content with whatsoever he obtaineth without effort, free from the pairs of opposites, without envy, balanced in success and failure, though acting he is not bound. Of one with attachment dead, harmonious, with his thoughts established in wisdom, his works sacrifices, all action melts away" (iv. 15,18-23). There, then, is the secret of the binding and the loosening there the teaching of the Lord of Yoga. How action may be done and yet no bonds thereby be made, how to combine activity and freedom, how to make action a way to liberation, these are the lessons of the *Gîtâ*.

How is this to be done? By yoga. There in two words is the answer. How to do it, how to act and not be bound, how to turn that which normally binds into the very means of attaining liberation, that is the lesson we are now to learn; and that "how" is yoga. By yoga. In no way else can it be done. These apparent contradictions only merge into harmony when yoga is understood. and therefore we naturally ask: What is Yoga? Who is the Yogî? By what means is Yoga to be obtained?

We receive the revelation of what is yoga from the teaching of the very Lord of Yoga Himself. What then is yoga, according to the *Gîtâ*?

It is better to take it first in the words of the *Gîtâ* itself, and we will define yoga as the *Gîtâ* defines it. Let your ordinary thoughts, for the moment, go. Do not confuse yourself, for the moment, with any ideas of yoga that you may have previously caught up. Listen, rather, to the words of the Lord of Yoga: "Here, to-day, behold the whole universe, movable and immovable, standing in one in my body, O Gudâkesha, with aught else thou desirest to see. But verily thou art not able to behold Me with these thine eyes; the divine eye I give unto thee—Behold my Sovereign Yoga" (xi. 7, 8). What is it? "Behold," He says, "My Yoga." "There Pâṇdava beheld the whole universe, divided into manifold parts, standing in one in the body of the God of Gods" (xi. 13). That is the supreme yoga—the vision of the union of the many seen in the One, the whole universe standing in one in the divine Body, that is yoga. The eleventh aḍhyâya is the very heart of the *Gîṭâ*, its essence. He who has no idea of the meaning of that aḍhyâya, he cannot reach yoga. It is its heart, its essence; everything leads up to that, and leads away from that. In the vision of the divine Form, in which everything is included, in that sovereign yoga, the one great liberating truth is told. This is the परमं वचः, the supreme Word (x. 1). This is the राजविद्या राजगुह्यं ज्ञानविज्ञानसहितं, kingly secret, kingly knowledge, wisdom and knowledge combined (ix. 2, 1). This is the आत्मयोगः, the Yoga of the Self, (xi. 47), or the very Self, the inmost heart of yoga. That is the supreme word and the highest secret: the many established in the One. Nothing less. And in the *Gîṭâ*, in shloka after shloka, this is insisted upon with re-iteration ever re-iterated; in *all*, making no exceptions; in so-called good, but also in so-called evil. If you cannot see that, yoga is not for you, you are not ready for it. "By this thou wilt see all beings without exception in the Self, and thus in Me" (iv. 35). "All evolves from Me" (x. 8), not only the good, the beautiful, the happy, and the harmonious; *all* evolves from Me. "I, O Gudâkesha, am the Self, seated in the hearts of all beings; I am the beginning, the middle, and also the end of all beings" (x. 20). All the practices that lead to yoga, which make a man harmonised by yoga, have only this for result, that being "harmonised by yoga, he seeth the Self abiding in all beings, all beings in the Self; everywhere he seeth the same" (vi. 29). How strange that sounds to some ears. "Everywhere the same." If only we might have a little more of the Self in the saint than in the sinner; if only the Self might be a little more in the good man than in the bad. "Not so," says the very Self Himself. "Seated equally in all beings, the supreme Lord, unperishing within the perishing—he who thus seeth, he seeth. Seeing indeed everywhere the same Lord equally dwelling" (xiii. 27, 28). It is put very, very, strongly so that no man may seek to escape it, or be able to misunderstand it. And even then, lest perchance the teaching might seem too strange, and exception should, in spite of all, be made, He declares: "The natures that are harmonious, active, slothful (सात्त्विका राजसा तामसा) these know as from Me" (vii. 12). There is no escape. You cannot put the slothful apart on one side and say: The Self is not in you. The slothful natures too, He declares, are all from Me. There is no good and no evil in essence, in the nature of things. All is part of the Supreme. We make things good or bad in relation to ourselves, by our ignorance, our folly, by our own passion, and we are here in order that, understanding at last the unity of all things, we may transcend good as well as evil, and rest finally in the Supreme. A hard doctrine, some people say. A dangerous doctrine, other people say. While all things are dangerous to the ignorant, nothing is dangerous to the wise. The unity is not seen in the lower stages, where it might be misunderstood or misconstrued. They see separateness, and not unity; they see the manifold, and not the One; they see the many, but not the standing in the one Body of the Lord. Each of them is sure that he is himself and no one else, that he is the actor, for he is entrenched in egoism. Right and well that he should be so entrenched for the time, for only thus will be learned the lessons that are necessary for the manifestation of the Self in him, that Self who dwells in each, waiting with infinite patience while the wheels of the vehicle learn their right place in the scheme of things.

The great Lord of Yoga does not fear to put the truth. Unflinchingly He declares once more, with that continual insistence of His, for those who are wise enough to read and to understand: "I am seated in the hearts of all, and from Me memory and wisdom, *and their absence*" (xv. 15). Not only, then, wisdom and memory, but also the absence of wisdom and the absence of memory. The 9th and 10th aḍhyâyas of the *Gîṭâ* are spent in nothing but in leading Arjuna up to the vision of the Supreme. One thing after another He declares to be Himself: I am this, I am that, I am the other. I am all Ṛiṣhis, and mountains, and rivers, and trees, and animals, for I am all. "A portion of mine own Self, transformed in the world of life into an immortal Spirit, draweth round itself the senses, of which the mind is the sixth, veiled in matter" (xv. 7). "When the Lord acquireth a body," it is written, the Lord Himself, when He taketh a body "and when He abandoneth it...... .....enshrined," when he takes it, "in the ear, the eye, the touch, the taste and the smell, and in the mind also, He enjoyeth the objects of the senses" (xv. 8, 9). Not many people now-a-days would dare to say that great word that "when the Lord taketh a body, He enjoyeth the objects of the senses." "The deluded do not perceive Him when he departeth or stayeth or enjoyeth, swayed by the qualities; the wisdom-eyed perceive" (xv. 10). Nay, lest people should still think, that after all, something might be left outside Him, He speaks of "men who perform severe austerities unenjoined by the Scripture", and declares of them : " Unintelligent, tormenting the aggregated elements forming the body, and Me also, seated in the inner body, know these demoniacal in their resolves" (xviii. 5, 6). So that these who torment even the outer body, torment the Lord Himself who is seated within. Rising into higher and higher flights of all-embracing Self-hood, He declares: " I also am everlasting Time...and all-devouring death am I, and the origin of all to come" (x. 33.34). " I am the gambling of the cheat, and the splendour of splendid things am I" (x. 36). "And whatsoever is the seed of all beings, that am I, O Arjuna; nor is there aught, moving or unmoving, that may exist bereft of Me" (x. 39). "As the one Sun illumineth the whole earth, so the Lord of the field illumineth the whole field, O Bharaṭa" (xiii.33). Such is yoga. The unity of all things, the many seen in One.

Who then is the Yogî? He is the man who, realising the Unity, lives it. He and he alone is the yogî. Such the declaration over and over again in this Yoga Shâsṭra, as to the man who is the yogî in the eyes of the Lord of Yoga, of Yoga's very Self revealed, as He is called (xi. 47). The yogî is the man who, realising the Unity, lives it. No one who does not thus realise and live it can be called a yogî, in the full sense of the term. Again we recall that phrase: "He that performeth such action as is duty...he is an ascetic, he is a yogî, not he that is without fire and without rites" (vi.1). It is not the outside garb of the man which makes the yogî; the yogî is not a man who wanders about with the cloth of a yogî, but "he that performeth such action as is duty, independently of the fruit of action." Now the man, who is the typical yogî is described in varied repetitions, and his characteristics are clearly defined. It is declared: "Equilibrium is called yoga" (ii. 48); only he who sees the permanent unity is stable amid the changing of the various transitory effects. He is skilful in outer activities: "Yoga is skill in action" (ii. 50). He feels no attraction for the objects of the senses, or for actions, and renounces the making of plans: "When a man feeleth no attachment either for objects of sense or for actions, renouncing the formative will, then he is said to be enthroned in yoga" (vi. 4). When He would define the perfect yogî, the man who has reached that perfection of Unity which means triumph, He declares it is: "He who through the likeness of the Self, O Arjuna, seeth equality in everything, whether pleasant or painful, he is considered a perfect yogî" (vi. 32). With care and elaboration in the sixth aḍhyâya, Shrî Kṛiṣhṇa works out this idea of a yogî: a yogî is one who is "established in unity" (vi. 31); who, his mind "fixed on the Self", (vi. 18), on the vision of the One present in all things, sees that even pleasure and pain are only phases of the manifestation of the One, and is "free from longing after all desirable things" (vi. 18), and thus reacheth "disconnection from the union with pain" (vi. 23). It is he "who is satisfied with wisdom and knowledge, unwavering, whose senses are subdued" and who is impartial (vi. 8, 9). With these objects he must meditate, for, in the rush and hurry of the outer world, he cannot realise the Unity, unless he withdraws from the multiplicity from time to time and looks at it from outside, "in a secret place by himself" (vi. 10); every man who would reach the vision of the Unity must, out of the many hours that he gives to work, to play, and to sleep, take a little time for solitude and meditation, until he is strong enough to meditate always in the midst of any whirl. Without this, it is idle to expect success. For inasmuch as we are not strong, but weak; inasmuch as we are not wisdom-eyed, but too often deluded; inasmuch as we are swayed by qualities, and think of things as separate, and permit one thing to give us pleasure and another thing to give us pain, instead of taking every thing painful and pleasant as experience, which can be used for the helping of the upâḍhis in which the Self is to be made manifest; inasmuch as that is so for all of us, we must take a quiet time in a secluded place, in which we sit apart by ourselves, and then, fixing the mind upon the Self, realise our unity with that Self, despite the whirling of events. We must follow the directions given by Shrî Kṛiṣhṇa (vi. 10-19), until we, "seeking the Self by the Self, in the Self" are "satisfied" (vi. 20); until we can find "the supreme delight which the Reason can grasp beyond the senses, wherein established," we shall not be "shaken even by heavy sorrow" (vi. 21, 22). Then shall we enjoy the "infinite bliss of contact with the Eternal" (vi. 28). And when all that is accomplished, when a man truly "seeth the Self abiding in all beings, all beings in the Self" (vi. 29), then he who, "established in unity, worshippeth Me, abiding in all beings, that yogî liveth in Me, whatever his mode of living" (vi. 31). That is the great truth of the true yogî. He may be a writer or a speaker, he may be a warrior or an agriculturist, he may be a philosopher or a merchant, he may be a King or a statesman, he may be a lawyer or anything else—it matters not. "He liveth in Me, whatever his mode of living," if he sees Unity in all things, all things in God.

That sums up, it seems to me, the whole essence of the thought that we have been following this morning "That yogî liveth in Me, whatever his mode of living." It is not what you are in your occupations, it is what you are in your mind; it is not your outer activities, it is the attitude with which you face the world; it is not what you *do*, but what in your feelings and your thoughts you *are*; it is that which determines whether you be a yogî or not.

On three paths they travel who seek yoga. I shall trace these paths, to some extent, to-morrow and the next day. You know that three are spoken of, the path of wisdom, the path of devotion and the path of activity, the three paths, each according to a temperament, the paths which are thought to be three but which blend into one, since the Self behind all temperaments is one. The Jñânî is he who follows the path of wisdom; the Bhakṭa or Tapasvî is he who follows the path of devotion; and the Kartâ is he who follows the path of action. But what did Shrî Kṛiṣhṇa say of these men, when he summed up this portion of His teaching on Yoga, contained in the sixth aḍhyâya? He said: "The yogî is greater than the ascetics, he is thought to be greater than even the wise. The yogî is greater than the men of action" (vi. 46). The perfect yogî is greater than the men on any one of the separated paths, greater than the men who are treading one or the other or the third of these three paths that lead to complete yoga; greater than the Jñâṇî, the Tapasvî, and the Kartâ, for he sums up their separate characteristics all within himself, in perfect equilibrium, and is none in particular because he is all together. He has learned right thinking, right desire, and right activity, and having thus become perfectly wise, active and devoted, he is greater than the predominantly wise, or devoted, or active; he has summed them up in himself. "Therefore become thou a yogī, O Arjuna" (vi. 46).

——:o:——

THE BHAGAVAḌ GÎṬÂ.

THIRD LECTURE.

METHODS OF YOGA. BHAKṬI.

BROTHERS:

YOU will remember that we considered yesterday the essence, the nature, of Yoga. But I spoke also of the means of reaching Yoga as one of the subjects of the *Gîṭâ*, and that is our special subject for to-day and for to-morrow also. How is yoga to be attained? We noticed, in studying its essence, that it consisted in the realising of the Unity; so that it was a very stable and well-equilibrated thing. The Yogî stands on the rock of the Unity, and from that all his activities are carried on.

Now as this stable centre, this equilibrium, is a terribly difficult thing to reach, it is no wonder that one of the very first questions that arose in the eager mind of the listening disciple Arjuna was this fact of the difficulty of attaining such a centre, the apparent impossibility of remaining quiet in the midst of the whirl. Hence we find him putting that celebrated question, which is repeated, I think, by each individual aspirant, as though this were some peculiarity of his own, special to his unfortunate self, which made the path more difficult for him than for any of his fellows. "This Yoga which Thou hast declared to be by equanimity, O Madhusûḍana, I see not a stable foundation for it, owing to restlessness; for the mind is verily restless, O Kṛişhṇa; it is impetuous, strong, and difficult to bend; I deem it as hard to curb as the wind" (vi. 33, 34). The answer comes promptly: "Without doubt, O mighty-armed, the mind is hard to curb and restless; but it may be curbed by constant practice and by dispassion. Yoga is hard to attain, methinks, by a Self that is uncontrolled, but by the Self-controlled it is attainable by properly directed energy" (vi. 35, 36). That is the constantly re-iterated answer of the Teacher of Yoga to this experience of the disciple constantly repeated. Each one of us knows it to be true that the mind is difficult to bend, hard to restrain, and the more we try to restrain it, the more vigorous appears the mind in its restless plunging; yet the Lord of Yoga declares that it is possible to attain equanimity, and He gives two words which are to guide the aspirant: constant practice and dispassion. You may remember a previous shloka in which He had said: "As often as the wavering and unsteady mind goeth forth, so often, reining it in, let him bring it under the control of the Self" (vi. 26). That is the "constant practice"; and without that, no possibility of equilibrium; and naturally so, because for thousands upon thousands and thousands of years the mind has been running out in every direction, and that running out of the mind is the mark of its development up to a certain stage. Where the mind ls in a low stage of development, it rests indifferent, sleeping, within the man, save when driven outwards by some potent physical craving. No progress is possible except by the going out of the mind, and this restless activity of the mind is necessary for evolution, necessary to carry the man on to a stage whence he can begin to work for equanimity. Constant practice then, the reining of it in and placing it within the Self, over and over again with untiring patience, with endless perseverance, that is the first step. Let the would-be yogî copy the magnificent patience which in the West is the characteristic of the scientist, that unconquerable perseverance with which, year after year, he will make the same experiment until the ultimate result is certain, and no doubts remain; that same magnificent patience is demanded from the would-be scientist in yoga, for yoga is verily a science and must be followed according to the law. But just because it is according to the law, it is certain. If it were not according to the law, then there would be no certainty of success, for you might constantly rein it in without result; but as it is the law that practice makes habit, and habit builds character, you may be sure that constant practice will gradually lead to the habit of equanimity, and this will become the fixed stability of character. Now the means for attaining this are not exactly the same for every man; and hence we find Shrî Kṛishṇa speaking of different methods, not dividing them very sharply the one from the other, passing, in fact, very rapidly sometimes from the one to the other. One shloka perhaps speaks of the one, the very next of the other, so that it needs a very careful study and a very clear insight in order that you may understand the directions given, and put each in its proper place. The three chief means of, or paths to, yoga are also called, in a secondary sense, yoga; the means are entitled yoga as also the end. These three are definitely named. There is the Yoga of Renunciation—the renunciation of desire: "harmonised by the yoga of renunciation, thou shalt come unto Me" (ix. 28). There is the Yoga of Discrimination—the yoga of knowledge: "I give the yoga of discrimination by which they come unto Me" (x. 10). There is the Yoga of Sacrifice—the yoga of action: "That of yoga by action, of the yogîs" (iii. 3). These are the three means, and we shall find, as we examine them, how perfectly is each adapted to its special end, and how, reaching that special end, the man finds that all the three have been acquired by him, and that along whichever of these three paths, as they are often called, he travels, he reaches the same goal. Only children, as was said with respect to the Sâṅkhya and the Yoga paths—only "Children, not sages, speak of the Sâṅkhya and Yoga as different; he who is duly established in one obtaineth the fruits of both" (v. 4). The wise know the three paths to be one, although the label placed upon each may differ, for reasons that we shall see in a moment.

First, consider the cycle of evolution, composed of two arcs, the descending and the ascending, the well-known Pravṛiṭṭi and Nivṛiṭṭi Mârgas, the path of forthgoing and the path of return. H. P. Blavatsky has laid continual stress on this "descent of the Spirit into Matter," and the subsequent ascent, and these two primary paths are necessarily trodden by all mankind in the long course of evolution; every human being is travelling along one or other of these two paths, of which may be used the phrase of Shrî Kṛiṣhṇa: "These are thought to be the world's everlasting paths; by the one he goeth who returneth not, by the other he who returneth again" (viii. 26). This is, of course, not the sense in which He used the words, and is not literally true of the Pravṛiṭṭi and Nivṛiṭṭi Mârgas, since a man may be on the Nivṛiṭṭi Mârga for many lives, ere he treads the final stage of it of which Shrî Kṛiṣhṇa is speaking, and returneth no more; but on it he is no longer going out, he is coming home, though home may yet lie far ahead. On the Pravṛiṭṭi Mârga the man is born again and again, brought to birth by desire, and born into the place suitable for the fulfilment of his desires, and each birth forges new links in the lengthening chain which binds him; on the Nivṛiṭṭi Mârga the man is born for the payment of the debts incurred by his past, and each birth breaks some link of the shortening chain which binds him.

On the Pravriṭṭi Mârga, consciousness is dominated, blinded, by matter, and constantly endeavours to appropriate matter and to hold it for using; as it becomes more familiar with its surroundings, it gradually appropriates more and more intelligently, and exercises more and more its selective powers; through experiences in matter it differentiates its own capacities, and its functions shew increasing specialisation; these functions slowly manipulate matter, and shape out organs for their own fuller expression; by the use of these orgains, the functions become more clearly marked, the cloudy becomes defined, the massive acute ; the vague "sensing" of the external world, in the earlier stages, becomes sight, hearing, touch, taste, smell ; sensations afford materials for cognitions, and consciousness unfolds. All this is necessary for its sovereignty over matter, and thus it treads the path of forthgoing. At last satiety begins to replace craving, and slowly, with many relapses into forthgoing, consciousness begins to turn inward, and a decreasing interest in the Not-Self permits the growth of an increasing interest in the Self. The man enters definitely on the Nivṛiṭṭi Mârga, the path of return, and all the instructions in the *Gîṭâ* are for the consciousness on that path. They are useless, inappropriate, even harmful, for one who is still on the path of forthgoing.

These two arcs of the circle of evolution give us the first main division of mankind into two great classes, those who are going forth and those who are returning, those who are differentiating themselves and those are unifying themselves. The first includes the vast, the overwhelming majority ; the second, at this stage of evolution, consists only of the few.

On each of these arcs, three sub-classes are seen, each distinguished by its temperament. By the word "temperament" I mean a type including an indefinite number of varieties, in which dominates one of the three aspects of consciousness, accompanied by its corresponding quality of matter, or guṇa. These are, as you well know, Jñânam, Kriyâ, and Ichchhâ, with Saṭva, Rajas, and Ṭamas—wisdom, action, will, with rhythm, mobility and inertia.

This line of thought carries us into that region of triplicity which is marked in our universe. You know how everywhere the triple nature of consciousness is recognised; how when Saguṇa Brahman is spoken of, He is declared to be Sachchiḍânanḍa; these qualities, reflected in human consciousness, are Kriyâ, Jñânam and Ichchhâ—the three aspects or functions of consciousness.* If instead of study-

*This is not the place to give a long explanation of the "why" of the transpositions of the members of the triplets, as given in the popular phraseology; to the Theosophical student the following diagram will suffice; the letters are the Initials of the qualities:

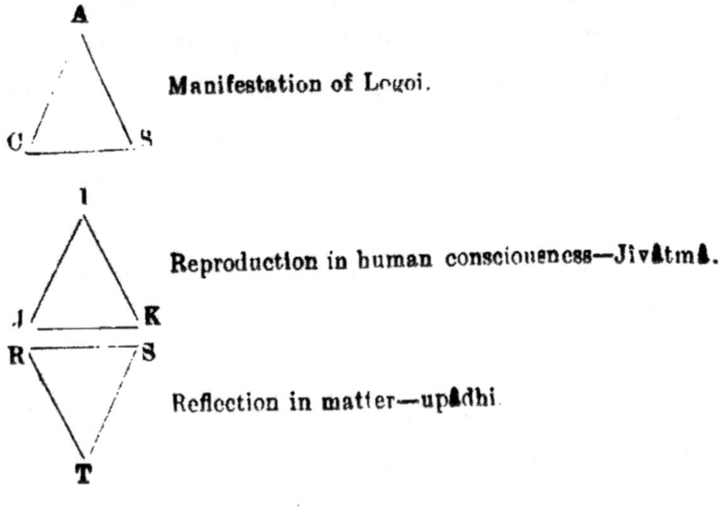

ing consciousness, we study the upâḍhis, the same triplicity presents itself, and we speak of them as corresponding to the three guṇas of Prakṛiṭi—Saṭva, Rajas, and Ṭamas. Everywhere we see that triplicity; but we see more than triplicity and must recognise that more as well; for unity underlies the triplicity, and wherever one function is specially seen, it must be remembered that the other two are present, ever connected with it, only temporarily hidden by its predominance, thus holding a secondary place. There is no atom of Prakṛiṭi which has not present in it always the three guṇas, inseparable and inseparate. You cannot say that one atom is sâṭvic, and one râjasic, and one ṭâmasic, for every atom contains the three equally. But when you think of combinations, when you think of molecules, tissues, organs, and bodies, then by the relative arrangement of the atoms, or the relative arrangement of the molecules, one quality may stand out dominantly, so that you may call the combination by the name of one of the three, and say: the combination is sâṭvic, râjasic or ṭâmasic. But you must never forget, when you speak of the combination as sâṭvic, that râjasic and ṭâmasic elements are also present therein. Although for the moment less prominent, they are none the less there, and are capable of being evoked; where the nature is said to be sâṭvic, there the râjasic and ṭâmasic elements are also present, and can be called out by appropriate stimuli; and where the dominant note is ṭâmasic, there the sâṭvic and râjasic are also present, and can be similarly stimulated into activity; and where the râjasic dominates, there are also the sâṭvic and the ṭâmasic. The oneness must never be forgotten; you must not be deluded by the triplicity. Nowhere do we get in the manifold a thing which is absolutely pure; everything is always mixed, all is present everywhere, but there is partial manifestation, and hence in manifestation there is multiplicity. May I, for a moment, put it in a materialistic way, using the analogy of the magnet. You all know that the magnet has positive and negative poles, and that along the central part of the magnet very little magnetism shows, so that it scarcely attracts or repels in the middle. Is it then that all the positive magnetism is at one end and all the negative at the other, and there is none in the middle? Not at all; but in the middle, according to an explanatory hypothesis, the positive and the negative currents so run as to counteract each other, while at each pole there is an uncounteracted current; hence at each pole a magnetic current naturally appears; at the positive pole, the positive electricity is, as it were outside, and at the other pole, the negative electricity is outside; always the current is there, circling round and round the molecules, and thus appears the variety which we think to be separation, but which is not really separation at all, but only a transitory appearance produced by arrangement of currents. Similarly the three aspects of consciousness are present in every individual, one or the other dominating in the way that I indicated.

Coming along the Pravṛiṭṭi Mârga, the three aspects of consciousness are called out into vivid growth, or rather unfoldment; all together are infolded, are present within, although not manifested; that fragment of the Self, the Jîvâṭmâ, has within itself all possibilities of divinity, but they are folded inwards, as in the seed are infolded all the possibilities of the tree that will grow therefrom. And very beautiful are the analogies in nature that you may see; for you may take a seed and, cutting it carefully, may see folded within it the three parts of the plant that shall be—the root that grows downward, the stem that grows upward, the leaves that spread upon either side; the plant in miniature is there, a wonderful microcosm of the future macrocosm of the tree; and so, in all other cases of embryonic growth; that way of nature, of folding together within that which has to be unfolded in the course of evolution, is repeated over and over again in the physical reflection, dominated by the seed of life which has come from Îshvara. Thus we have here in each Jîvâṭmâ, that enters upon the Pravṛiṭṭi Mârga, the three functions, or aspects, of consciousness present, and all have to be made active, to be manifested, to be brought into functional activity. In order that that may be, the world exists. It exists only for the sake of the Jîvâṭmâs unfolding within it, and every detail of the world is planned with nicest care and finest wisdom, in order that these divine powers may be drawn out of their embryonic condition and manifested in their full glory as the result of the labour of the universe.

We find then that the world is crowded with objects, in order that those objects, attracting and repelling each other, by their collisions and separations may bring about the evolution of form and the unfolding of jîvâṭmic powers; every object, in turn, is a stimulus to the evolution of others, and itself receives a stimulus from others, for the unfolding of the Self within all. Stones and trees, animals and men, devas and asuras, they are all affecting each other and being affected by each other, a continual interaction, a perpetual mutual modelling and influencing, and on that the progress of the unfolding depends.

In order to awaken that aspect of consciousness that is called Ichchhâ, the world is filled with desirable and repulsive objects. The giver of the objects of desire, Shrî Lakṣhmî, consort of Viṣhṇu, the great type of Prakṛiti, is the one in whose hands lies the treasure of desirable things, by which this aspect of consciousness shall be stimulated, strengthened and unfolded. Forget not that Lakṣhmî is the consort of Viṣhṇu, that Desire is the servant, the devotee of Wisdom. Ichchhâ must be called out by the presence of desirable objects on every side, so that, going out after them, it may gradually become potent, and its mighty energy within consciousness may be awakened. But the aspect also of Jñânam must be called out. That will be stimulated into activity by the cravings of desire, by the longing for desirable objects. And in all its earlier evolutions it will not be the lord of desires but their servant; it is not yet Jñânam in the higher sense; it is still in its lower manifestation. And lastly, there must be evolved also the Kriyâ aspect, activity, the power to affect the external world. Ichchhâ is the change within consciousness, the tendency to impel towards the obiects of desire; and Jñânam is that which mirrors within itself the objects; and Kriyâ is that which goes forth to obtain, to grasp, to seize; and all three are wanted that consciousness may become perfectly manifest.

Moreover, each of these has two aspects—a

higher and a lower, belonging respectively to the Pravṛiṭṭi and the Nivṛitti Mârgas. Fundamentally each remains the same, but the manifestation of each changes according to the direction of the path. And we shall see presently that the change consists in the lower, when it has been evolved to its full power, becoming the higher by changing its attitude, and all the strength which has been gained in the lower world changes its direction and goes forth towards the Supreme. Thus, in the *Devî Bhâgavaṭa*, is Durgâ said to change with Her attitude; turned away from Her Lord, She is Prakṛiṭi; turned towards Him, She is one with Him, is Mahâḍeva.

Pause then for a moment on the Pravṛiṭṭi Mârga. There desire is very good. Without desire, no progress; without desire, lethargy, coma. Interesting to notice that Ichchhâ has as its special correlation in the world of matter the ṭâmasa guṇa. The guṇas, like the aspects of consciousness, have a lower and a higher; the lower ṭamas is sloth, quiescence, the higher is peace, stability, equilibrium; the inertia of matter corresponds with the absolute quietness, the peace, of the Supreme. There are the higher and the lower poles of matter. In the higher a perfect stability, in the lower a moveless inertia. In the forthgoing path that inertia has to be overcome, and it is overcome by arousing in consciousness attraction to and repulsion from desirable and repellent objects; desire awakens, and overcomes sloth, and passionate longing conquers the obstacle placed in its way by the inertia of matter. Not too soon must that lower aspect of desire be renounced. For, if too soon it is renounced, progress is stopped. If too soon it is given up, the tâmasa quality re-asserts itself and lethargy takes the place of activity. The man of the world, the worldly man in the full sense of the term, *should* be full of desires. And so also with the other aspects of consciousness. It is well that the aspect of Jñânam, which is wisdom, takes on the form of Vijñânam, discriminative knowledge that separates, that divides. The knowledge of the separated must precede the knowledge of the One, and until this function of consciousness has mirrored the manifold, there is no hope of its realising the nature of that manifold, and of its seeing through the manifold to the Unity that underlies. The more perfectly that aspect of consciousness discriminates, separates, and classifies, the more thoroughly does it begin to understand; and so in science, which is the expression of this lower aspect of Jñânam, the lower pole of Jñânam, science is, above all, the idea of difference, and then the idea of classification, a stage of unification. Until you know the different, you cannot know the One. Oneness makes no impression upon the consciousness until difference has aroused the consciousness into awareness of that which is not itself. If you are surrounded by moveless air, you are not conscious there is air; only when there is the movement of wind, do you know that you are surrounded by the ocean of the atmosphere. One colour only would be no colour, for you would see nothing else, and the idea of colour could not arise. Only when the differences of colour appear is the colour-sense evolved. Happiness could not be felt, were it not for its other aspect, suffering, for only by the change from pleasure to pain, from joy to sorrow, do you evolve the knowledge of either, and in that the possibility of transcending both. Hence this scientific stage, this lower pole of Jnânam, is one which must be worked through on the Pravṛiṭṭi Mârga, and the more perfectly it is developed, the more ready will consciousness be for the great change of direction, that presently will come.

The third aspect of consciousness, Kriyâ, activity, that also must be brought out, stimulated in every direction, making desire restless, making the mind restless, and making the body restless, rushing here and there in continual hurry and continual turmoil. It is all very good. The rush, the whirl, the worry—it all means growth. Time enough to begin to regulate, when you have got something to regulate; until the energy is there, no useful control is possible, for there is nothing to control; the stronger the manifestation of the aspects and the qualities, the greater the hope for the man.

Now, I know that that is not the way in which the subject is generally put, and we will come to the other side in a moment, but everything in its place and its order. The man who is bursting with desires, that sweep him away and carry him off; the man whose mind is very active, quick and restless, examining, observing and tabulating, classifying, making inductions and deductions; the man whose body is full of activity, which, if it wants to move, has to run instead of walking, so great is the necessity for motion, that is the man you can make something of in the future. I don't say that such a man is attractive for those who see only the outer-side of the qualities; but he is the man with possibilities, the man in whom something is unfolded, and in whom therefore there is something upon which to work. If you want to build a house, you first want bricks; and though the bullock-drawn carts which bring and throw down the bricks are not very beautiful and attractive, they are all necessary for the work of the architect, for the building of the bricks into the form of some beautiful edifice. The man who goes to sleep every moment, what fitness has he for the strenuous labours of the higher path? Believe me, Îshvara would not have designed all this turmoil, if it were not the best way to the goal, for Love and Wisdom guide the Universe; it is out of the very men who have trodden the Pravṛiṭṭi Mârga so eagerly that those who are to tread the Nivṛiṭṭi Mârga first will be found. It is right to grasp, right to appropriate, right to hold; all these are the valuable efforts of consciousness on the Pravṛiṭṭi Mârga; by these the consciousness is unfolded, by these the bodies are developed, by these the organisation is shaped, by these the vehicles are fabricated, which are needed for the future purposes of the Jîvâtmâ. Even if you take one of the most unlovely products of modern civilisation, the man who has piled up millions upon millions of coins by the destruction of countless homes, by the impoverishment of countless families, you find that that man has developed power of will, that man has developed concentration of mind, that man has developed an activity that knows not weariness, that seeks not rest from labour; and although his object be a very poor one, yet in pursuing it he has developed qualities which, when the object is changed from an ignoble to a noble one, will make of him a mighty power in the world.

But now let us see how the change is brought about. We find that Shrî Kṛiṣhṇa speaks of men who worship for the sake of reward; a new tendency is implanted in the human soul by this worship, and though we may not think that worship for the sake of reward is a very lofty thing, yet we can only take men as they are, not as we fancy that they ought to be. The three twice-born castes, so often mentioned, respectively symbolise one special type of nature; at the stage we are considering, the men in each are moved by desire, and the desire is shaped by the special aspect of consciousness as dominant in each. In the Vaishya, dominated by Ichchhâ, activity is stimulated by the ḍharma of accumulating the objects of desire; in the Kṣhaṭṭriya, dominated by Kriyâ, activity is stimulated by the ḍharma of splendour, sovereignty, power. In a Brâhmaṇa, dominated by Jñânam, activity is stimulated by the desire for Svarga, the desire for the joys of heaven. In each, activity is motived by desire, and for this worship is enjoined in the exoteric cult. It is said in the second adhyâya: "With desire for self, with heaven for goal, they offer birth as the fruit of action, and prescribe many and various ceremonies for the attainment of pleasure and lordship" (ii. 43). These are the ceremonies, performed under the stimulus of desire to enjoy sovereignty, lordship, pleasure, and lead to birth as a Kṣhaṭṭriya, in which state profit and pleasure are legitimate, hand in hand with the performance of duty. Of the Brâhmaṇa, it is said: "The knowers of the three—the three Vedas—the soma-drinkers, the purified from sin, worshipping Me with sacrifice, pray of Me the way to heaven; they, ascending to the holy world of the Ruler of the Shining Ones, eat in heaven the divine feasts of the Shining Ones" (ix. 20). And so also there is the typical Vaishya, who desires success in action; of him it is said: "They who long after success in action on earth sacrifice to the Shining Ones; for in brief space verily in this world of men, success is born of action" (iv. 12). See how in worship thus offered there lies hidden the beginning of a change. Desire is the motive, desire for the personal self; but where that motives one dominated by the Jñânam aspect, there the object is lifted into a more distant and subtler realm, it is the feast of the Ḍevas, the joys of the world of the Shining Ones. Sacrifice must be offered, desire for physical objects must be curbed, and sacrifice of them must take place, in order that the subtler pleasures may be enjoyed. For physical pleasure and lordship and sovereignty, a Kṣhaṭṭrîya must make sacrifice and perform ceremonies, and thus on him is imposed a partial curb, which trains him, forces upon him some self-denial, while he enjoys lordship and sovereignty, until at last they satiate him. And so a Vaishya is bidden also to sacrifice some of his wealth, in order that success in action may be his, and he is taught to make sacrifice to the Devas, so that the very longing for success may serve as a subtle means of disuniting him from the very desire which is his stimulus. How wise it all is. There is no hurry; there is plenty of time. Let all the desires grow and flourish, that the man may become strong; and begin to curb them by the principle of ceremony and sacrifice; but still let them strive towards their goal; still let them have their proper stimulus; joys of heaven instead of those of earth, wide lordship instead of smaller powers, great wealth instead of narrow means. The object is kept as a stimulus as long as it is wanted, and the taste for objects is encouraged, but is slowly curbed, restrained, brought under control, by the principle of sacrifice; and as this goes on life after life, the Self at last grows a little weary of this constant outward running, and in that period of weariness everything seems transcient, sapless, empty; heart-sick disappointments come, sorrows come, frustrations come; the man who is grasping powers grasps them, and finds them burdensome; the man who is longing for knowledge gains it, and has his heart laid desolate, made empty; the man who is toiling to win some great success gains it, and finds his castle of success is only a prison. Thus gradually the Jîvâtmâ, unfolding within, realises that all these objects are not enough to satisfy him; he has tasted until he is sick of taste; he has enjoyed until he is satiated with enjoyment; he has studied until the burden of knowledge becomes wearisome, and endless detail, unknown reaches, stretch infinitely beyond. The Self grows weary of this repeated experience; that is the turning point, and at this turning point, a momentary dispassion grows out of weariness; it is not the real Vairâgya, which is the fruit of knowledge, but a passing Vairâgya, which is the fruit of disgust, and in that moment, standing at the junction of the two paths Pravṛiṭṭi and Nivṛiṭṭi—at that turning-point in the long journey, weariness overpowers the pilgrim-soul, and in that weariness, a subtle change goes on within the consciousness, and from seeking the lower pole it slowly turns and begins to rise up to the higher. "Even relish—for the objects of the senses—turneth away from him after the Supreme is seen" (ii. 59). Each still keeps its characteristic quality, but by the change in the direction in which it is travelling, this characteristic quality assumes its higher character and is gradually transformed. Each of the three aspects simply changes its object; in the change of the direction of the whole consciouness, Ichchhâ, desire, the lower pole of which is kâma, becomes desire for the Self, the Supreme, which is the higher pole, bhakṭi. Vijñânam, the lower pole, which realises the separateness of all outer objects, becomes jñânam, the wisdom that knows the One. Kriyâ, instead of manifesting at its lower pole as activity for objects, manifests at its higher, and becomes yajña, sacrifice. Thus, on the Nivṛiṭṭi Mârga the three have changed their names but not their quality, and we have bhakṭi, we have jñânam, we have yajña—these are the higher manifestations, these the higher poles of the three aspects of consciousness, and so we find Shrî Kṛishṇa saying that at this stage: "Some by meditation behold the Self in the Self, by the Self" *i.e.*, in the way of bhakṭi; "others by the Sânkhya yoga", *i.e.*, by the way of jñânam; "and others by the yoga of action," *i.e.*, by the way of yajña (xiii. 24). They have come to the place where the means of yoga are to be taken up and practised; and still on the Nivṛiṭṭi Mârga we see the three paths within the one; and according to the dominant temperament will be the path which there is chosen, and each has its own appropriate yoga; for the Ichchhâ aspect, there is the Yoga of Renunciation; for the Jñânam aspect, there is the Yoga of Discrimination—not now between object and object, but between the real and the unreal, the transitory and the eternal. And for the third, the Kriyâ aspect, we have the Yoga of Sacrifice; when all action is done as sacrifice, as we saw yesterday, its binding quality melts away.

Now all is changed. We have to study the three aspects as they are seen on the Nivṛitti Mârga, each with its own appropriate yoga, the practice of which is the treading of the special path. We shall take up first the path belonging to the aspect of Ichchhâ, and see how the man who is of this temperament must guide himself if he would tread the Nivṛiṭṭi Mârga. We now at once meet the teaching so familiar to you all as regards desire, that which is the guide of the aspirant, the Yoga of Renunciation. When Arjuna, turning to his Teacher, asked him: "Dragged on by what does a man commit sin, reluctantly indeed, O Varṣhṇeya, as it were by force constrained?" (iii. 36) what was the answer? "It is desire, it is wrath, begotten by the quality of mobility; all-consuming, all-polluting, know thou this as our foe here on earth" (iii. 37). Hence He says to His pupil: "Slay thou, O mighty-armed, the enemy in the form of desire, difficult to overcome" (iii. 43). On this Path of Renunciation, on the Nivṛiṭṭi Mârga, the lower aspect of Ichchhâ, desire, becomes the great enemy of man. And so again the Lord says in His wisdom: "Affection and aversion for the objects of sense abide in the senses; let none come under the dominion of these two; they are obstructors of the path" (iii. 34). But what is the man to do? He has been developing these things all along; affection and aversion have been his motive powers; how then is he to change, and look on them as his foes, his enemies that have to be slain? They have been his friends, his companions during youth, his relatives; how empty will life be when they are slain; on the Kurukshetra of the soul they are his foes, arrayed against him. How shall he fight? The first step is a step of forcible abstention from the gratification of desire. "As a tortoise draws in on all sides its limbs, he withdraws his senses from the objects of sense" (ii. 58). The man, realising the futility of constant enjoyment followed by suffering; realising that all contact-born delights are verily wombs of pain (v. 22); realising that the pleasure which at first is nectar later becomes poison (xviii. 38); recognising all this, what shall he do? The first step is to forcibly hold himself back by the mind from the objects of desire; this he can do, for "greater than the senses is the mind" (iii. 42). And so it is said that from the abstemious dweller in the body, the objects of the senses gradually turn away (ii. 59). And this for a very simple reason. Because in every object of desire is hidden a fragment of the Self, which allures another fragment, awaking therein desire for union; but when that fragment of the Self begins to desire union with the Self and not with the outer husk, and deliberately rejects the husk, the Self within the object withdraws that object and neutralises its alluring influence; thus the rejection of the object by the man is answered by the withdrawal of the alluring object by the Lord, who lives within the objects of the senses. Thus may the objects refused be truly said to "turn away from an abstemious dweller in the body".

Then the second step is taken. The man is only holding himself back by force. His desires are longing again to plunge into sense-delights, for "relish" remains, but with iron hands he holds them back; desire is changed into will, and instead of being drawn from outside, it is being guided from inside. Out of that forcible abstention, out of that turning away from the objects of desire, there comes to the abstemious dweller in the body, in the midst of these frustrated longings, a vision of the Supreme, of the supreme delight beyond the senses (vi. 21). When the vision of the Supreme dawns upon the abstemious dweller in the body, then relish itself turneth away; desire dies, conquered by the mightier desire, slain by the bhakṭi, which is the perfection of that temperament which has sought all desirable objects. With the vision of the Supreme, who becomes the Object of desire, the Object of devotion, all lower objects lose their attracting power, and have no longer force of allurement to draw the man away; a mightier attraction has been felt, that of the Self unveiled, whereas before the Self was veiled within the husk of the desirable object; that overmastering desire takes away all taste for the fleeting objects of the moment, and then comes the regular practice of the Yoga of Renunciation : " That which is called renunciation know thou that as yoga, O Pâṇdava ; nor doth any one become a yogî with the formative will unrenounced......When a man feeleth no attachment either for the objects of sense, or for actions, renouncing the formative will, then he is said to be enthroned in yoga" (vi. 2, 4). " Harmonised by the Yoga of Renunciation," says the Lord, " thou shalt come unto Me" (ix. 28). "Sages have known as renunciation the renunciation of works with desire" (xviii. 2). Giving up desire is renunciation, is the Yoga of Renunciation, the Bhakṭi Mârga, and it becomes an easy path when once the Supreme is seen.

The Yoga of Renunciation has many points in common with the Yoga of Sacrifice, and is very often confused with it—the two in fact are so often interblended in the teaching, that it is easier to take them together than apart. Yet there is a difference which marks out the one from the other ; for in the first, the Yoga of Renunciation, you have as motive power the love for the Supreme, devotion, bhakṭi, desire fixed on that one object ; all else loses its power, and, as it were, becomes out of focus, is not clearly seen, and is not cared for. He "abandoneth, O Pârṭha, all the desires of the heart, and is satisfied in the Self by the Self" (ii. 55). Happiness is found alone in the one Object, and the glimpses of that give to life its savour. Then he "goeth to Peace" (ii. 64), On the other hand in the Yoga of Sacrifice, the Karma Mârga, what is changed is the motive of action; the change is not in the direction of desire, cousciousness dominated by Ichchhâ, but in the spirit in which action is done, consciousness dominated by Kriyâ. It is sacrifice, action done as sacrifice, which is the characteristic of the Karma Mârga.

Now in order that the path of devotion may be trodden, a man must make up his mind to abandon the gratification of the desires that spring up within his heart, and the best way is the daily effort to train himself to become gradually indifferent to pleasure or to pain. Do not try to be at once completely indifferent, but when a pleasure comes, do not allow yourself to enjoy it to the full, for you are no longer wishing to develope the power of desire for objects, but to turn yonr desire to the Supreme. When a suffering comes, do not allow yourself to be overwhelmed by the suffering, but remember that it is only a passing phase in the midst of pleasure. Keep the memory of pain in the midst of pleasure, and keep the memory of pleasure in the midst of pain. Thus is it possible to take "as equal pleasure and pain" (ii. 38). Blend them together in thought. Remember that the one and the other are only two sides of the same aspect of the Self, the aspect of

Ichchhâ; neither of them is permanent; both of them are transient, and they succeed each other as do night and day, coming and going continually: "The contacts of matter, O son of Kunțî, giving cold and heat, pleasure and pain, they come and go, impermanent: endure them bravely, O Bharața" (ii. 14). See them together, as one aspect of the Self, and learn to blend them in your daily life; in so blending try to see the elements of pleasure in pain, try to recognise the elements of pain in pleasure. Mingle them in thought and life, until either becomes equally attractive with the other, until you no longer shrink from what is painful, nor long for what is perishable; but when the pleasurable is present, you take it, and when the painful is present you take it; but if the pleasurable is absent, you long not for it, and if pain is absent you do not desire it (xiv. 22). You have to learn how to remain balanced in the surge of pleasure and in the surge of pain. "The knower of the Eternal ......neither rejoiceth on obtaining what is pleasant, nor sorroweth on obtaining what is unpleasant" (v. 20).

Next, it must be remembered that on this path of devotion there are two chief dangers that touch the man, after the foe of desire has partly been slain —or rather transmuted; for there are tremendous risings and fallings in the nature whose temperament is dominated by the aspect of desire. At one moment the man is very elated, at the next moment he is correspondingly depressed—very, very glad over a pleasure, very, very sorry over a pain. He must reach the middle point. He must stop the extreme elation, and with the stopping of that elation, he stops also the extreme depression. He must gradually let the waves of pleasure and pain play round him, while he himself stands steadily on the unchanging rock of devotion to the Lord; then neither the waves of pleasure nor the waves of pain can sweep him off his feet, firmly based upon the rock; he does not cease to feel them, for the feeling is necessary for work in the future, but he ceases to be so strongly affected by them as to lose his balance. That is one lesson for the Bhakṭa.

The other chief danger that threatens him, as we may see in the history of all great devotees, is the danger lest, growing for a while out of the desires and realising a longing for the Supreme, he should at times, by weariness and weakness, sink back into the lower desires he had thought he had renounced, and imagine that he is longing for the Supreme when he is really longing for the satisfaction of desire, and is seeking pleasure even on the Path of Renunciation. "How few there are," said a great Christian Saint, "who are willing to serve God for naught." Hence arises the phrase that you find in many books of devotion, that a man must be naked to tread this path; as it is said in the *Imitation of Christ*, the devotee "must naked follow the naked Jesus." He must look for nothing. The same idea comes out in some of the stories of Shrî Kṛishṇa, as in the taking away of the garments of the Gopîs, and in the Kalki Avaṭâra, where He must fight weaponless, with his naked hands. It is a warning, in the shape of an allegory to the devotee, to beware how he enters on that path of loftiest emotion while still the garments of the lower emotions cling round his limbs; for the lower emotions are a snare to the man who is treading the path of emotion purified and sublime. He must guard himself rigidly and carefully, and must be sure that the body is his slave, else the body may betray him in a critical moment, and he may fall for a while from the path. And so it is written, that he may avoid it: "Let him sit, aspiring after Me" (vi. 14); "Having made the mind abide in the Self, let him not think of anything" (vi. 25). How often is the phrase repeated: "He who thinketh upon Me, not thinking ever of another" (viii. 14). "With the mind clinging to Me" (vii. 1). "On Me fix thy mind; be devoted to Me; sacrifice to Me; prostrate thyself before Me" (ix. 34). "Merge thy mind in Me, be My devotee, sacrifice to Me" (xviii. 65). It is to those, "who worship Me alone, thinking of no other, to those, ever harmonious, I bring full security" (ix. 22). "He, the highest Spirit, O Pârṯha, may be reached by unswerving devotion to Him alone" (viii. 22). Such is the Bhakṯi Mârga, where the appropriate yoga is that of renunciation. It is an unselfish and perfect devotion to the Lord, as the one centre of love and of service, the hope for union with the Lord as the one motive for all that is done. In the heart of such a devotee wisdom springs up in process of time. "To those, ever harmonious, worshipping in love, I give the yoga of discrimination, by which they come unto Me" (x. 10). "The man who is full of faith obtaineth wisdom" (iv. 39).

Naturally wisdom must come where there is perfect devotion, for what is it that blinds wisdom? It is desire—man is blinded in his thought, confused, because of attractions and repulsions around him; his thoughts are coloured by desire; he sees everything through the coloured atmosphere with which desire encircles him. He thinks things to be right because he longs for them, and he thinks things to be wrong because he is repelled by them; and only when all this colouring of desire has been destroyed can the clear white light of the wisdom of the Self shine through to the man, undistorted and undimmed. To the man who is perfectly devoted inevitably will wisdom come and to him also right activity; for what should be his will in action save the will of the Lord he loves? He unites himself in thought with the Object of his devotion; all that he does is not done by him but by his Lord through him, and he is only the channel whereby the power of the Lord flows down to the world of action; he is ever fixed in meditation, in his heart thinking only of Him, and through that heart, opened to the Supreme, there flow down floods of blessing to the world of men, for the devotee is a channel for his Lord. To such a man all else becomes indifferent; he need no longer think of what men call duties: "Abandoning all duties, come unto Me alone for shelter" (xv. iii. 66). "He goeth by renunciation to the supreme perfection of freedom from obligation" (xviii. 49). That is the message to the devotee. And he abandons duty, because, with the heart purified from all desire, his Lord through him performs all action that is duty, and he has no further concern with it in any way; he may abandon duty because he has no desire, and because the power of the Lord flows through him as through a channel to the world. Such is the man who is a true devotee: "He from whom the world does not shrink away, who doth not shrink away from the world," who "is pure, expert, passionless, untroubled," "taking equally praise and reproach, silent, wholly content with what cometh" (xii. 15, 16, 19). Of a man who is equal in pleasure and in pain, unconscious of desire or repulsion, a man who looks on all the qualities as moving, himself moveless, united to the heart of the Lord, of such a man it is written : he is "best in Yoga" (xii. 2), "He, My devotee, is dear to Me" (xii. 16).

———:o:———

THE BHAGAVAḌ-GÎṬÂ.

FOURTH LECTURE.

DISCRIMINATION AND SACRIFICE.

BROTHERS:

WE have to deal to-day, however imperfectly for lack of time, with the two other forms of preliminary yoga, belonging to the two aspects of consciousness which I left untouched yesterday. You will remember that, after sketching the aspects of the paths of forthgoing and return, I took up a special preliminary path suitable for the Ichchhâ aspect of consciousness, and we find that in that aspect which manifests in the lower world as desire, the desire for objects is changed into desire for the Supreme, devotion, and this leads a man to the perfection of yoga.

To-day we have to consider the remaining two forms of preliminary yoga, the Yoga of Discrimination, connected with the jñânam aspect of consciousness, and the Yoga of Sacrifice, connected with the kriya aspect. I must ask you in following my hasty sketch of these, to take it simply as an outline into which the details must be fitted by your own study and by your own living, for especially, perhaps, is the first part of our subject, the Yoga of Discrimination, difficult for those who have not studied deeply the constitution and nature of man. And yet for those in whom the jñânam, the cognitive, or knowledge, or wisdom, aspect is predominant, this is the form which leads to the ultimate yoga, to union with the Supreme.

Now with regard to this aspect, the aspect of wisdom, there is one great danger that assails the would-be Sage, for to him, above all others perhaps, the senses are the avenues of danger, and yet these senses have been hitherto his avenues of knowledge, and he must strive to thoroughly control these before anything of the nature of even the preliminary yoga becomes possible for him. And so we find Shrî Kṛiṣhṇa declaring as regards this path for the man who would become wise: "O son of Kunṭî, the excited senses of even a wise man, though he be striving, impetuously carry away his mind. Having restrained them all, he should sit harmonised, I his supreme goal; for whose senses are mastered, of him the understanding is well-poised" (ii. 60, 61). And in order to show that not the senses in general only, but even one sense is a source of danger: "Such of the roving senses as the mind yieldeth to, that hurries away the understanding, just as a gale hurries away a ship upon the waters. Therefore, O mighty-armed, whose senses are all completely restrained from the objects of sense, of him the understanding is well-poised" (ii. 67, 68). Of desire "The senses, the mind and the reason are said to be its seat......Therefore, O best of the Bharaṭas, mastering first the senses, do thou slay this thing of sin, destructive of wisdom and knowledge" (iii. 40, 41).

The opening of the great teaching of the Yoga of Discrimination is the first note which is struck in the *Bhagavaḍ Gîṭâ*. "Thou grievest for those that should not be grieved for, yet speakest words of wisdom" (ii. 11). Now it is said in the introduction to the practice of the *Gîṭâ* which is called *Gîṭâ* Karâḍinyâsa, that these words: "Thou grievest for those that should not be grieved for," are the Bîjam of the *Gîṭâ*. You know the force of that word Bîjam, Seed. A bîjam is a sound, word or sentence to be pronounced at the beginning of a manṭra, in order to bring about a desired effect. It varies with individuals, and the particular sounds which are given as the Manṭra-bîjam give to the manṭra its peculiar, its special, force, so that a general manṭra becomes specialised by giving to it a certain bîjam, or seed. In that bîjam is the very essence of the whole manțra. The manțra-fruit grows, for the individual, out of these seed-sounds that precede the repetition of the manțra. These words: "Thou grievest for those that should not be grieved for," are said to be the bîjam of the manțra of the *Gîțâ*. They are its essence, they reveal its object, they give to it its special significance. The whole of the *Gîțâ* is wrapped up in these, as the plant in the seed. They are also the opening of the teaching of the Yoga of Discrimination. "Thou speakest words of wisdom," said the Teacher, for Arjuna's argument had been eminently reasonable argument, as I pointed out to you the other day. His objection to the slaying of his kindred was perfectly natural; his feeling that royalty was too dearly purchased by slaughter was quite a laudable feeling; his shrinking from shedding torrents of blood was a thing that should be praised in any thoughtful and compassionate man. Yet the Teacher said: "Thou grievest for those that should not be grieved for." But why? "The wise grieve neither for the living nor the dead." Now, why is it that the wise do not grieve either for the living or for the dead? The answer to that lies in the teaching of wisdom, the path of the true Jñânî, the teaching which is scattered throughout this discourse of the Lord of Wisdom. He begins, you remember, by those marvellous shlokas which rapidly sketch out the reason for not grieving which is to be expounded in the remaining teaching of the Wisdom. The dead should not be grieved for because there is no such thing as dying. All that is real can never cease to be, and that which can lose being has never really had it at all (ii. 16). "This Dweller in the body of every one is ever invulnerable" (ii. 30). No weapon can cleave him, no injury can touch him (ii. 23-25). He is unborn, undying, ancient, constant, perpetual, eternal (ii. 20), and knowing him as such "thou shouldst not grieve" (ii. 30). That is the first hint of the great teaching that is to follow, that is to be made clear, definite, precise, so that Arjuna may understand the nature of the world and the nature of the man within the world; for knowing that, understanding that, founded, established in wisdom, it will become impossible for him to grieve, as grieve the ignorant and the foolish. He will be established in the Self and all doubt will flee away.

Let us see then what is this Yoga of Discrimination, this profound teaching of the Wisdom, which is to elevate the pupil who becomes the Sage above all the sorrows of the world.

It is first of all the teaching of the nature of the world, of the nature of the Lord of the world, and of the various parts of His nature, which we distinguish here as higher and, lower, Supreme Lord and the World. And it is intended specially for those who are mentioned by Arjuna in his question as to the best kind of yoga : "Those devotees who ever harmonised worship Thee, and those also who worship the Indestructible, the Unmanifested, whether of these is the more learned in yoga?" (xii. 1) And the Lord answered: "They who with mind fixed on Me, ever harmonised worship Me, with faith supreme endued, these, in my opinion, are best in yoga. They who worship the Indestructible, the Ineffable, the Unmanifested, Omnipresent, and Unthinkable, the Unchanging, Immutable, Eternal, restraining and subduing the senses, regarding everything equally, in the welfare of all rejoicing, these also come unto Me. The difficulty of those whose minds are set on the Unmanifested is greater; for the path of the Unmanifested is hard for the embodied to reach" xii. 2-5). And we find Him elsewhere mentioning those whose natures prompt them to tread this harder, this more difficult path, as one of the divisions of the "righteous ones who worship Me" (vii. 16). "Of these," says the Lord of Wisdom, "the wise, constantly harmonised, worshipping the One, is the best; I am supremely dear to the wise and he is dear to Me. Noble are all these, but I hold the wise as verily Myself" (vii. 17, 18). Now you may think in linking these two passages, in one of which it is said that those who worship full of faith are best in yoga, and in the other of which it is declared, that the wise is best, for "I hold him as verily Myself," that it is a little difficult to find out which is really the better of the two. The answer to that is simple: that a way is better or worse for a man according to his temperament; that for a man like Arjuna, full of emotion and of passion, the best way was the way of devotion; but for him, who is by temperament inclined to wisdom, for him the way of wisdom is the best. Just as the devotee reaches union with his Lord, so the wise who is "verily Myself" shall come unto Him by knowledge; for the Lord is Wisdom and Emotion and Action, and each is best in its place, and each offers a road, one for each of the three temperaments among men. Each one is best for him who naturally belongs to it, "for the path men take from every side is mine" (iv. 11).

Let us listen to the Lord teaching the way of wisdom, and understand that knowledge is the foundation of right conduct.

First of all, He explains His own constitution, and He tells us it is three-fold—the Supreme Spirit clothed in Spirit and Matter, the Self garbed in Nature, which is dual. The teaching of this three-fold constitution is scattered through many passages, and each adds something to our knowledge, as we find when we bring them together. In summarising these passages, I draw them from widely different parts of the *Gîțâ*, in order to unite them into one coherent and intelligible whole. His lower nature, the Aparâ Prakṛiṭi, is: "Earth, water, fire, air, ether, and reason also, and egoism—these are the eightfold division of my nature. This the inferior" (vii. 4, 5), the Aparâ Prakṛiṭi. Keep that idea clearly in mind, distinct from all else for the moment; the lower nature of the Lord, the lower Prakṛiṭi, includes the whole of the manifested, visible, phenomenal, nature; it is all part of Him; all manifestation of the physical universe, all manifestation of the subtle universe, all phenomena, the appearances that on every plane of nature form the beings of the plane, form the outer objects of the plane, all are summed up in one great generalisation: "They are His inferior nature." Ever remember that though they are the inferior nature, they are still part of the Lord. They are not to be separated from Him, as though independent; they are not to be separated from Him as though antagonistic. They are part of His nature; they are His inferior nature, and the "knowledge of... my perishable nature" (viii. 4), is the Aḍhibhûṭa, knowledge concerning the elements, which are built into forms. Another note which comes out, over and over again in the *Gîțâ*, with respect to this lower nature is the word "manifested." Wherever the manifested is spoken of we have to do with the lower nature of the Lord, the Aparâ Prakṛiṭi. Before we go further into that, let us see what is the second division of His nature, the Parâ Prakṛiṭi, sometimes called Ḍaivaprakṛiṭi, that which He describes, continuing that shloka that I read: "Know my other nature, the higher, the life-element, O mighty-armed, by which the Universe is upheld" (vii. 4). This Parâ Prakṛiṭi, this higher nature, this life-element, the Jîvabhuṭa, the Purusha of the Sâṅkhya, is contrasted with the other elements. This is the higher nature of the Lord. The knowledge of this, the science of the life-giving energy, of the life-side of nature, is the Aḍhiḍaiva, the knowledge of the Shining Ones, who are the life-channels, the channels of His life, called in modern science the energies of nature. Thus we have two great sciences to study on the path of knowledge, one concerned with His "perishable nature," and the other with His "life-giving energy." The first is the manifested, the second is called the unmanifested; but it is the lower unmanifested (see viii. 20, xv. 17), a point of immense importance, for, losing sight of it, the whole teaching becomes confused. Truly it is the life pervading all things and upholds the universe. "By Me all this world is pervaded in my unmanifested aspect" (ix. 4); it is unmanifested, hidden behind the veil of matter, but it is still the lower unmanifested, and it is not the highest division of His nature.

Again we find Him declaring that "there are two energies in this world, the destructible and the indestructible; the destructible is all beings, the unchanging is called the indestructible" (xv. 16). Once more we have two significant words that we must bear in mind, the lower, the destructible, the manifest, that is what we call the phenomenal; and the higher, the indestructible, unmanifested, that is what we call the life that pervades all nature. These again are spoken of by Him as "Matter and Spirit" (xiii. 19); Matter the lower, Spirit the higher; but "know thou also that Matter and Spirit are both without beginning" (xiii. 19); for both being of the nature of the Lord, forming the inferior and the higher divisions of His nature, they share the endlessness and the unbeginningness of the Lord; they are both to be considered as "without beginning."

It is these which, in very truth, form what we call "Nature." The two together, the two "energies" (of xv. 16), these, taken together, are Nature. And they show forth a constant turning of the wheel of life; the manifest, the lower, passes into the unmanifest, the higher, and the unmanifest, the higher, gives out again the manifest, the lower, at the beginning of a new Kalpa, a new world-age; you have revolving before you this great wheel of life, manifest from the unmanifest into the unmanifest again. In the beginning of the world-age the manifested appears. At the end of the world-age the manifested disappears into the unmanifested. "All beings, O Kaunțeya, enter my lower nature at the end of a world-age: at the beginning of a world-age again I emanate them. Hidden in Nature, which is mine own, I emanate forth again and again all this multitude of beings, helpless, by the force of Nature "(ix. 7. 8).[1] I pause on that for a moment, because the words—if you forget certain other shlokas in the *Gîțâ* which explain them—may confuse you in your own study. Notice the phrase "enter my lower nature," and you at once say that the words "lower nature" must mean Aparâ Prakŗiți. But when the Lord contrasts Himself with Nature, then the two divisions, hitherto spoken of as lower and higher, relatively to each other, both become lower, relatively to Himself. This is put still more plain-

---

1 The latest researches of Science on the nature of the atom throw a vivid light on this picture of appearing and disappearing universes. The atom, we are told, is probably a "knot" or "strain" in the ether, and atoms may appear, when the ether is subjected to strain and disappear when the strain is relaxed. Suppose the ether, the true ether, is the "life-element;" suppose the atoms are the "inferior nature;" then with the strain, caused by the will of the Lord, out of the life-element would come the inferior nature, out of the ether the atoms, and when the will relaxed, into the life-element the inferior nature would return, the atoms into the ether.

ly in another shloka which I shall now refer to, in order that any possible misunderstanding that lies hidden may be cleared away. He had already explained it, before He uttered that statement which I just read, for He had said in the preceding discourse: "From the unmanifested all the manifested stream forth at the coming of day: at the coming of night they dissolve, even in That called the unmanifested. This multitude of beings, going forth repeatedly, is dissolved at the coming of night; by ordination, O Pârṭha, it streams forth at the coming of day. Verily, therefore, there existeth, higher than that unmanifested, another unmanifested, eternal, which in the destroying of all beings is not destroyed. That unmanifested, 'the indestructible,' it is called. It is named the highest path. They who reach it return not" (viii. 18-21). So again, after the words: "There are two energies in this world, the destructible is all beings, the unchanging is called the indestructible," we read: "The highest energy is verily Another, declared as the Supreme Self, He, who pervading all, sustaineth the three worlds, the indestructible Lord. Since I excel the destructible, and am more excellent also than the indestructible, in the world and in the Veḍa I am proclaimed the supreme Spirit" (xv. 16-18). Again He says: "Under Me, as Supervisor, Nature sends forth the moving and the unmoving; because of this, O Kaunṭeya, the universe revolves" (ix. 10). And again: "Supervisor and permitter, supporter, enjoyer, great Lord, and also the supreme Self; thus is styled in this body the supreme Spirit" (xiii. 22). Another explanation is given in aḍhyâya xiii, which deals with the Field and the knower of the Field. The Field is nature, and when the Field is described we find both Matter and Spirit entering into it, for both of these make the Field; the Knower of the Field is the Lord. The Field is described: "The great elements, Individuality, Reason and also the Unmanifested"—that is, the unmanifested into which all the manifested goes at the end of a world-age, and out of which it comes at the beginning—"the ten senses and the one and the five pastures of the senses; desire, aversion, pleasure, pain, combination [the body], intelligence, firmness, these, briefly described, constitute the field and its modifications" (xiii. 5, 6). The field is nature, and the higher and lower are the body of the Lord. And He, the Great Lord, the Supreme Self, in this body of the Universe, is styled the Supreme Spirit (xiii. 22). He is the Knower, not the Known, He and He alone is the Object of Wisdom. Now it is written of this Supreme that He is ever unmanifest: "Those devoid of reason think of Me, the unmanifest, as having manifestation, knowing not my supreme nature, imperishable, most excellent" (vii. 24).

When, following out this thought, we dwell upon it, holding all these passages in mind, the idea comes out clearly and definitely, and we see the great Triplicity: He who is called "another unmanifested," "verily another;" He who is called "supervisor;" He who is called "the supreme Self," "The supreme Spirit," Purușhoțțama, rules all, clothed in a dual nature composed of Matter and Spirit, Prakŗiți and Purușha; these, taken together, make up nature; and the Lord of nature is greater than nature. Matter and Spirit form the wheel of life, but the Lord sitteth above the wheel, unchanging; the play of Matter and Spirit, of the Aparâ and Parâ Prakŗițis, goes on; the changes continually recur of appearance of one from the other, and disappearance into that other again; behind these stands the unchanging Lord, and these two together are His Mâyâ, which the deluded are unable to pierce through, by which the ignorant are blinded, so that they see not through them to the Lord who is beyond (vii. 25, 27). Think, then, of this first pair of opposites, Matter and Spirit, as the veil of the Lord Himself. Think of Him, the unchanging, as ever behind the twain, supervisor, Lord of Nature, Lord of Mâyâ, this universe but the veil of His ineffable glory, and He, behind it, the Indestructible, the Ineffable, the Unchanging, the Eternal, the Supreme. That is what is shown to us in the teaching of the *Bhagavaḍ-Gīṭā*, as regards the relation of the Lord to His world. "Having established all this universe with one fragment of Myself, I remain" (x. 42).

Before taking our next step, let us for a moment pause and ask how all this teaching is to help us in our realisation of the Unity. For we find ourselves in the face of a triplicity, not of a Unity; we see the Supreme Lord and His unmanifest and manifest nature. How is this to teach us to grieve neither for the living nor for the dead? How is this to comfort us with regard to our own nature, in which we to see both Matter and Spirit, and we are told that both of these appear and disappear. Because Puruṣhoṭṭama, the Supreme, He is verily Another, the highest, eternal, and He is the innermost Self of man. Did you think that you were only parts of nature? Did you think that in you there was only this double Prakṛiṭi, the higher and lower? Did you imagine that in you there was only the manifestation of nature, not the very essence of the Lord? Nay, the Lord Himself abides within your bodies as in the body of the universe, the Indestructible, the Supreme; Puruṣhoṭṭama Himself is enveloped by the bodies of men. You are not merely the nature which he speaks of. You are not merely the Parâ and Aparâ Prakṛiṭis. These are your bodies, as they are His body, and you are part of the Supreme Himself, verily Himself, "a portion of mine own Self" (xv. 7) as He declares. "A portion of mine own Self, transformed in the world of life into an immortal Spirit," such are you. He is not then so far away. He is not far from any one of us. Unmanifest He may be, as regards the Parâ and Aparâ Prakṛitis, but He cannot be unmanifest to Himself. He is not really hidden from us, because He cannot hide from Himself, and to think that He can be hidden from us, who are Himself, is the subtlest Mâyâ of all Mâyâs, is illusion. He is our innermost Self, and the very heart of our being. If there is anything a man may know, surely it is his own innermost Self, that which lies behind Spirit and Matter alike, that which is himself—this surely a man may know.

Therefore is it Wisdom to realise that the Supreme Self is "seated equally in all beings," and "he who thus seeth, he seeth" (xiii. 27); the Lord is in the heart of every man, and the Lord is the innermost nature of each.

Suddenly, by one great illumination, we find ourselves elevated above nature, and in the Supreme, who is the Lord of nature. We share His innermost nature, He is our innermost Self. What need then of fear, of sorrow, of delusion, for those who have known the Oneness? That is the Wisdom.

To know the Knower, and to know that the Knower is ourselves. That is the great lesson of the wisdom of the *Gîtâ*. Over and over again He says it, that we may not feel that the One is far away. "The eternal seed of all beings" (vii. 10), He calls Himself. "The life in all beings" (vii. 9), He calls Himself; there is no hesitation, no doubt, no whittling away of, no shrinking from, this uttermost truth. He and He alone is the life within everything; by Him everything lives. If men hate each another, they "hate Me in the bodies of others and in their own" (xvi. 18); if men torment bodies, they torment "Me also, seated in the inner body" (xvii. 6). There is no escape from the fulness of this glorious truth.

Yet is He ever hidden from all eyes that cannot pierce through Nature. He declares: "Nor am I of all discovered, enveloped in my creative illusion," (vii. 25), my yoga-mâyâ. How is it that the One is to be seen in all varieties of forms? Whence spring they, these endless combinations and permutations, hidding the oneness of the Self? They are all guṇa-mayi, guṇa-made, consisting of the guṇas, the three qualities of matter, of the lower nature, which, continually combining into endless varieties, delude outer observation; so He declares of these: "All this world, deluded by these natures made by the three qualities, knoweth not Me, above

8

these, imperishable. This divine illusion of Mine, caused by the qualities, is hard to pierce; they who come to Me, they cross over this illusion" (vii. 13, 14). None is exempt from the sway of the qualities: "There is not an entity, either on the earth or again in heaven among the Shining Ones, that is liberated from these three qualities, born of matter" (xviii. 40). Yet must the wise pierce through them in order to reach the Lord. And all the natures are from Him: "The natures that are harmonious, active, slothful, these know as from Me" (vii. 12). As I said before, they are all of the body of the Lord, are part of Himself. Piercing the known to know the Knower, that, alone, is Wisdom.

Let us analyse this illusion. There is first the primary pair of opposites, attraction and repulsion, attraction of the nature of Spirit, and repulsion of the nature of Matter. Attraction is the effect of the one indivisible and unmanifested life, hidden in innumerable forms, and tends to unify. Matter, whose essence is multiplicity, is ever trying forcibly to divide, to become manifold, and again more manifold, continually. And the manifold is continually dividing, and subdividing, and yet again subdividing, so that finer and finer become the subdivisions, and the infinite variety of a universe is found. In that infinite variety is mirrored the indivisible Lord. Because of the subdivisions and mutual limitations of material forms you must needs have infinite variety. How otherwise should the infinite be mirrored in any real sense at all? No one fragment of this constantly dividing matter can mirror the whole complete. Infinite Beauty must be mirrored in an infinity of beautiful objects. The sea, the sky, the field, the mountain, the desert, the plain, and the crowded town, all these with all their varied elements reflect the rays of the one sun, Beauty, and in their multitude, their totality, lies their perfection, for thus only can they mirror forth the One out of whom they spring. So with all else in the world; it is in the totality of the subdivided that you can see mirrored the Indivisible, the One. Since Matter is thus ever dividing, it is easy to see why it has come to be the type of that which opposes the liberation of Spirit, which is unity. We understand why, in this first pair of opposites, Matter and Spirit, Matter becomes apparently the enemy, the foe, at certain stages of human evolution. So long as Spirit is going outwards with Matter, and Matter is indefinitely dividing itself and thus lending itself to the constructive power of Spirit, so long Matter is very good, and is a friend. The repulsive element, which is of the very essence of Matter, and brings about the necessary subdivisions, is the quality needed for the unfolding of Spirit, and hence is good. But when the Unity is to be aimed at and realised, when the universe has trodden half its course, and the second half is to be reintegration into Oneness, instead of differentiation into heterogeneity, then the principle of division is seen as the enemy, then the repellent forces are seen as foes, then it is that what was good becomes evil. That becomes evil which has in it the principle of separation, because the time for separation is over, and the time for working towards unity is come. And so, in regard to this preliminary pair of opposites, Matter and Spirit, repulsion and attraction, both of which, being of the Lord, are infinitely good, in the course of evolution comes a change, and repulsion becomes evil, a source of trouble, because against the changed current of the divine Will. From this first pair of opposites stream forth two lines of emotion, one of love, tending to nnify, and one of hate, tending to divide; these are "the pairs of opposites, sprung from attraction and repulsion" (vii, 27), the root pair from which outspring all other pairs. This gives us a science of ethics, and looking thus at the world we understand what are Right and Wrong, and when and why Right is Right, and Wrong is Wrong. This is given us by the Lord of Wisdom in the sixteenth aḍhyâya of the *Gîtâ*, in which out of this primary pair of opposites, from which, as just said, all other pairs of opposites are developed, we find that two sets of moral qualities are given, one called divine, because belonging to the Daivaprakṛiṭi, and the other called demoniacal, because belonging to the Matter side of nature, the Bhûṭa,. or elements. These become opposed, in the course of evolution in the world of men, as divine and demonaical, where really there can be no conflict, since they are both the body of the One; but in time they are opposed, when humanity has to climb into conscious unity. All that tends to division, all that is of hatred, all that is of separation, takes on the aspect of evil to the evolving man. He must triumph over it, he must resist it, for he has to climb out of it, and therefore he must identify himself with the divine, and struggle against the separative instinct which is born of the past.

Such is the great Yoga of Wisdom, growing out of a real understanding of the nature of the Field, the nature of the Knower of the Field, and their relation one to the other (xiii. 2). And therefore it is said that the wise worship "the One and the manifold everywhere present" (ix. 15), for they know the manifold is only the One in disguise, that the manifold is only the One in manifestation. Where that wisdom has been gained, there liberation is at hand: "I will again proclaim that supreme wisdom, of all wisdom the best, which all the Sages having known have gone hence to the supreme perfection" (xiv. 1); of this it is written: "Better than the sacrifice of any objects is the sacrifice of wisdom, O Parantapa. All actions in their entirety, O Pârthâ, culminate in wisdom" (iv. 33). This wisdom burns up all actions "as the burning fire reduces fuel to ashes" (iv. 37); this is the supreme purifier: "verily there is no purifier in the world like wisdom" (iv. 38). Now you can see why the jñânî grieves not. Why should he grieve in all this play of mâyâ? In all this changing nature why should he grieve who realises his one-ness with the changeless Self? Therefore is it written, as the seed of the whole exposition: "The wise grieve neither for the living nor for the dead." It is easy to see also why it is written that the wise look equally, with an equal eye, upon all: "Sages looks equally on a Brâhmaṇa, adorned with learning and humility, a cow, an elephant, and even a dog, and an outcaste" (v. 18). The wise look equally on all, they see no difference, because they see the Self dwelling equally in all, as much in the outcaste as in the Brâhmaṇa, as much in the dog as in the cow; they see the Self in all, and they who thus see, and they alone, are wise. All others are deluded by outer appearances; all others are under the dominion of mâyâ. Those who have transcended mâyâ see no difference, for all are the bodies of the Lord. Such a man has reached "the highest state of wisdom" (xviii. 50), and "becoming Brahman, serene in the Self, he neither grieveth nor desireth; the same to all brings, he obtaineth supreme devotion unto Me. By devotion He knoweth Me in essence, who and what I am; having thus known Me in essence, he forthwith entereth into the Supreme" (xviii. 54, 55). "In them, wisdom, shining like the sun, reveals the Supreme...they go whence there is no return, their sins dispelled by wisdom" (v. 16. 17).

There is a third form of preliminary yoga, in addition to that of devotion and that of discrimination. It is Karma Yoga, the Yoga of Action. But what action? The action which is sacrifice; and so it may be fitly called the Yoga of Sacrifice. Now this preliminary yoga of action, or of sacrifice, is sometimes simply called yoga, "yoga by action, the yogîs" (iii. 3), without any prefix, and this for the reasons that I gave you in the earlier lecture, when speaking of activity and of the perfect yogî; for this shows out into the world many of the characteristics which belong to the final activity of the perfect yogî; hence yoga by knowledge and yoga by action are said to form the two-fold path. Now in this path of yoga by action there are many difficulties, and very serious difficulties; and the chief of these is the understanding of action itself. "What is action, what inaction? Even the wise are herein perplexed. Therefore I will declare to thee the action by knowing which thou shalt be loosed from evil. It is needful to discriminate action, to discriminate unlawful action, and to discriminate inaction; mysterious is the path of action. He who sees inaction in action and action in inaction, he is wise among men, he is harmonious, even while performing all action" (iv. 16-18). These are the initial difficulties that are going to surround the Karṭâ; he has to find out what ought to be done and what ought not to be done, to discriminate right action from wrong, right activity from wrong activity; and the first thing he has to remember is: "Thy business is with the action only, never with its fruits" (ii. 47). The fruits belong to the Lord who guides; the result goes to the Lord, when the action is done as sacrifice, for man has nothing to do with a sacrifice, save with the making of it, and that which is the fruit of sacrifice is taken up by the higher powers and directed to necessary ends. And so thy business is with the action only. Realising that, a man should "perform right action" (iv. 8); "constantly perform action which is duty" (iii. 19). What is duty? What is right action? These are the questions to which we want answers, if we are to tread the path of action safely, and not be continually bound by our activities, unconsciously grasping after fruit. The Lord tells us very definitely what is right action. It is "acting in harmony with Me" (iii. 26). You have to discern the divine Will in evolution before you can perform right action; but, while seeking for ever clearer vision, you may follow some preliminary rules. Perform the duties that come in your way, and are imposed on you by karma, individual, family, social, national, for these are placed there for you by the Lord. A right actor does not go rushing about seeking for activities; he takes the activity that comes naturally in his way, and strives to perform it perfectly, remembering in every function he discharges that he is the Lord in action, and is not truly the doer of the action (iii. 27). In this effort to understand, wisdom is developed, for in the attempt to discriminate between right action and wrong action—that is, often, the duty, or action, of somebody else, in doing which there is always danger (iii. 35)—effort evolves faculty. The effort will of itself lift up the actor into the regions of clear vision, and will strengthen the mind and guide him towards wisdom.

Another simple rule is that of the activities that come in your way, and are useful, that is duty which is within your capacity; the right actor measures his own strength, and does neither too much nor too little. But suppose that many useful things come in your way and are within your capacity, but that they are more than you are able to fulfil; they may seem to have a claim on you, may appear as duties, but you have neither the strength nor the time to do them all? Then the knowledge that you are limited by time as well as by capacity marks out for you your sphere of duty. As much of all these as you can do according to your capacity and according to your time, so much is your duty. But if, trying to do more than you can do perfectly, you grasp at a number of things that you have not time to finish, you are going beyond right action; you find that your time is limited and the "duties" appear to he unlimited, and then you have to realise that that which you have not time to do is not your duty, but the duty of another, and, once more, "the duty of another is full of danger". The actor slides into danger, if he tries to do more than he has the time or capacity to do. You may say: "There is so much to do, so many claims on me and my time, so many actions that need to be performed, and so many things to be done." Quite true. But you are not the only person who can do things. You are not the solitary individual, endowed with all powers, all capacities, and all time, that the whole world should depend upon your activity, and that nothing should be done to which you do not put your own small hand. That is a mistake which so many of us make, and which has to be avoided in treading the path of action. That which we have not time to do is not our duty, and if we do it, we are keeping another man out of his duty and forcing him into idleness. The result of this lack of understanding what is duty is that one man is always in a frightful rush, and leaves half his works unfinished because he has no time to complete them; and another man is lying idly by, with empty hands, with nothing to do, because the other man has greedily taken everything for himself. That is not the "action which is duty", for the Lord is Time, as much as everything else, and the limitations of time are the limitations set to each of us by the Lord. If you have not time to do a thing which needs to be done, be you sure that the Lord will find for Himself other actors and other hands, for He has hands everywhere (xiii. 13), and not only in connection with one single body. This is the great lesson for the active, because the active are often the cause of inaction in others, of idleness, of sloth, and of all the qualities that hinder men in their progress. Over-activity is not the path of action, it is the path of the world. A difficult lesson, I know, for an active man, because a part of his activity is a sense of capacity; he is able to do things, and he often forgets to measure the time as well as the power. But both are of the Lord, and both have to be considered. And this I know to be true from my own experience, for many things crowd round me, crying out: "Do me, attend to me;" and there are many more than I can do, and I used to try to do them all and failed, and never felt as though I had done any one single thing thoroughly well. Then I realised that the Lord could do very well without me, and was not dependent on one particular body in which He, after all, was the Actor and not I, and that He had many bodies in which to act. And then I realised that to do what I could do well, and to leave the rest undone, was the path of wisdom in action. And always I have found that when that which for lack of time is not one's duty is left on one side undone, others at once come in and take it up, and thus the whole work is better done when one person does not try to monopolise it.

How shall an active man learn this lesson? He learns it by that great truth: "I am not the doer." "The Self, deluded by egoism, thinketh: 'I am the doer'" (iii, 27). That is not so. The wise man says: "I do not anything, should think the harmonised one, who knoweth the essence of things; seeing, hearing, touching, smelling, eating, moving, sleeping, breathing, speaking, giving, grasping, opening and closing the eyes, he holdeth: 'The senses move among the objects of the senses'" (v. 89). "I do not anything." That is what is meant by inaction in action (iv. 18). Like his Lord he sits above the qualities, and lets the qualities work. He looks on, and when he realises: "I am not doing anything," then all right activity is done through him, and all things move smoothly on their appointed course. The great lesson for the doer is: "I am not the doer." And this the man should repeat as he performs actions. There is only one Doer, the Lord Supreme, and the human doer is only one of His hands, a hand put into the world of men to perform certain separate work; it is not the business of the hand to think as to how all work that lies everywhere shall be done, but only how best to do the particular task which has to be done. And if you can think of yourself only as the hand—a hand able to think, so as to find out the best way, then you will lose in every case the grasping after an impossible multiplicity of work. If a man wants to paint, he need not hold in his hand at the same time a paint-brush, a pen, a pencil, with perhaps a plough, a hammer, an axe, as well; but he should have a brush when he wants to paint, and when he wants to plough he must take a plough in his hand; when he wants to write he must do so with a pen, and when he wants to draw he must do so with a pencil. One tool at one time, that is the method of wisdom in action. Do perfectly whatever you do, for remember you have to re-produce in your work your Lord's perfection, and it is better to do one thing perfectly than to do a hundred things imperfectly. In order that this may be so, man must not only lose attachment to the fruit of action (iii. 19), but he must do all action as sacrifice (iii. 9). That great law of sacrifice which upholds the Universe must finds its embodiment in the active man. All nature is upheld by sacrifice. In the 4th aḍhyâya the Lord gives a long description of the various kinds of sacrifice which men perform. All these men, He says, are knowers of sacrifice (iv. 30), and all action must be done for the sake of sacrifice.

What is the Law? It is that all beings must live by the sacrifice of the lives of others, and, therefore, that every being, as he becomes self-conscious, must be ready to repay his debt by the sacrifice of himself. It is not only in men that the Law is found. It is found among stones, vegetables and animals. The stone is broken up for vegetable food; the vegetable is broken up for animal food; animals prey upon animals, and the strong devour the weak; men prey upon men, devouring each other physically first, as food, then in other ways. The Law of Sacrifice is everywhere present in nature because the Lord is the Lord of Sacrifice, and the first sacrifice is the sacrifice of Himself. He is the Puruṣha, out of the parts of whose body the whole Universe is made. Self-consciously in man the Law of Sacrifice must gradually be learned. Man, as he evolves, sees that he lives by the sacrifice of other lives, and he says to himself: "The stones die for me to support the vegetable kingdom; the vegetables die for me, that my body may be supported; the animals yield their lives for me, ever yoked to my service and trained to my work; my body is the result of countless acts of sacrifice, and it only continues to live by the continual sacrifice of others; innumerable lives are built into the body that I wear, so that my body is the altar on which myriads of lives are sacrificed. Then, in common justice I must repay all these sacrifices by the sacrifice of myself, and thus turn the wheel of life. I must give myself up for others. I must live for other men. I must live for the animal kingdom, the vegetable kingdom, and the mineral kingdom, all of which can be evolved more rapidly by my help; because I am the result of sacrifice, I must be a sacrifice."

Next, a man learns to discriminate as to the lives sacrificed to him, and he seeks to support his own life at as little sacrifice from others as he can possibly exact. And so, out of the myriad lives that offer themselves to him, he choses those that are least developed in consciousness for building up his own framework, and the more conscious lives he seeks to train and discipline, for their own helping as well as for his service, and he seeks to evolve himself and them, and thus the Law of Sacrifice becomes his law of life. He associates himself with it in every action of his life. On the Nivṛiṭṭi path he is paying back the debts which on the Pravṛiṭṭi path he contracted. Therefore that which is his duty, that which is due from him, he ever strives to do, paying back his debts. He thus sacrifices the result of all his actions, which are not his but his Lord's, and thus he becomes perfect in action; for only the man who does not care for fruit is able to perform action perfectly. Does that sound strange when we see that all men are moved to activity by desire for the fruit of action? When we see men who lose desire for the fruits of action become supine, inactive, slothful? But a new motive for action has arisen in the true actor, who, thinking only of His Lord and of himself as the channel for the Lord, cares nothing for what is called success or failure, since the only success he knows is the doing of His will, and the only failure he can imagine is going against that will which is the law of his life. What the world calls success or failure, what matters that to him? They are both on the path of duty. Why should he trouble himself whether the building he erects is a building which is going to shelter man directly from the outer storm, or whether it is only providing a strong foundation on which some greater building of the future shall be raised? Foundations of buildings are made out of the broken materials of other buildings. Even when you want physically to build a new thing, you must get a quantity of broken bricks and stones, and lay them to begin with as the foundation; and many things which are the temples of the future are having their foundations laid to-day out of the apparent failures of those who are working for the Lord. Why then should they mind? What failure is there if they are providing Him with what He wants for His building in the future? And inasmuch as the true actor knows that he himself, surrounded by mâyâ, is often confused and blinded, that which he thinks is good and part of the plan may really not be in the plan at all, and he may often be in error in the way he plans it and the fashion of his work, he works ungrudgingly and without attachment, and when he builds up something which seems to him to be very beautiful and very useful, and it all falls to pieces around him, he is not moved, he is not troubled, he does not mind; he is willing that it should be broken up, if it is not what the Lord requires for His building. What is it to him, who is the hand of the Lord, if the ruins of his fine buildings make the foundation of the true Temple? If the metal he prepares is not needed, he gladly throws it all into the smelting pot, sure that only the dross will be burnt up, and the gold remain. The dross itself has its own place, and will also work in with the broken stones and bricks for a foundation, though not for the finished structure. And so he lives, and so he works, and thus working, without desire, he can work perfectly. He can catch sight of every sign of his Lord when desire does not blind him. He can catch the lightest whisper, when he is deaf to the clamour of the outer world.

Along this path of action, by the yoga of sacrifice, he also becomes free. "Whatsoever thou doest, whatsoever thou eatest, whatsoever thou offerest, whatsoever thou givest, whatsoever thou doest of austerity, O Kaunţeya, do thou that as an offering unto Me. Thus shalt thou be liberated from the bonds of action, yielding good and evil fruits" (ix. 27, 28). Action also thus leads to liberation, and to perfect yoga, union with the Supreme.

But one Lord is the Object of all devotion; but one Lord is the Object of all wisdom; but one Lord is the Source of all activity. One Lord, and therefore one humanity; One Lord, and therefore oneness through the whole of the body of the Lord; One Lord, one Life, one Brotherhood, that is the outcome of our study. The wise will help with their wisdom, the busy with their activity, the devotees with their love, and they will all blend together and make one perfect body. When the universe has done its work, and the day of rest has dawned, then shall the glory of the body of the Lord shine forth in all the varied temperaments, in all activities, and all thoughts, and all desires; these are the cells and tissues that build up that glorious Body. We shall then see that out of one universe rises, in this Body of Light, the Lord of another universe, and we, parts of His Body, shall work with Him in that new universe more perfectly than we have worked here. Thus on from age to age, from universe to universe, and where, I say again, where is grief, where delusion, when thus we have seen the Oneness?

———:o:———